MISS DIANNE' SJAZZ AND BLUES KITCHEN

A Novel

BOOK ONE

By

Jan Alan Eglen PhD

AI Content Disclosure

Miss Dianne's *Jazz and Blues Kitchen* (Book One) is an original work conceived, directed, substantially developed, reviewed, and approved by Jan Alan Eglen.

In accordance with publishing-industry standards and distribution guidelines concerning artificial-intelligence transparency, the author discloses that generative AI tools were used during the development of this manuscript. Their use included editorial support, developmental assistance, plot and structural architecture, character-continuity review, setting integration, operational detail, narrative organization, and prose refinement.

The creative vision, characters, world-building, core narrative decisions, and final approval of the manuscript remain those of Jan Alan Eglen. The completed work is the author's original intellectual property.

Featuring: The House Band

For the women who built the room.

For the men who understand why it matters.

For the music that makes it safe to tell the truth.

"There is always a door that isn't on the floor plan.

The architect knows this. The builder knows this.

The woman who commissioned it knows this best of all."

Table of Contents

A Note On The Building 6
Prologue: The Lot 7
Tamara's Mountain 12
Dianne's Voids 15
Rafi's Notebook 18
The Band: Who They Really Are 26
Chapter One: Poinciana 49
Chapter Two: Thursday 87
Chapter Three: What The Tunnel Knows 106
Chapter Four: The Distribution List 123
Chapter Five: Thursday Returns 147
Chapter Six: Who's Keeping Watch 169
Chapter Seven: Celestine's Thursday 186
Chapter Eight: The File 202
Chapter Nine: It's Not My Time 219

A Note On The Building

The building at the corner of M Street and Georgetown Drive in Georgetown, Washington D.C., was constructed in 1887 and operated for ninety-one years as a private gentlemen's club whose name does not appear in this novel because it does not deserve to.

It was vacant for eleven years.

It was acquired in the spring of the year this story begins by a limited liability company whose registered agent was a real estate attorney in Dupont Circle and whose beneficial owners were, on paper, two women from New Orleans with impeccable taste and a fifteen-volume business plan.

The building has four floors above ground and two below.

The two below do not appear in any document filed with the District of Columbia. This is not an oversight. The District has, in its long institutional memory, learned to be incurious about certain basements.

The architect who designed them is no longer in private practice.

The machinist who built certain components of the door hardware works in a shop that does not advertise and does not need to.

The building is, by every measure available to the public, a restaurant. It is also several other things.

This novel is about what happens when those things are required to be the same thing simultaneously — and what it costs the people inside when they are not.

Prologue:
The Lot

It was Tamara who saw it first.

This was consistent with the general architecture of their friendship — Tamara seeing, Dianne understanding, the two functions so naturally distributed between them that neither had ever thought to question the arrangement. Tamara's eyes moved fast, the legacy of a woman who had spent the formative years of her life reading terrain at sixty miles an hour, calculating the line through a course before her body committed to it. She saw things early. She saw things whole. It was the gift the mountain had given her before it took everything else, and she had kept it the way you keep the things that survive catastrophe — carefully, gratefully, with full knowledge of what they cost.

What she saw, on a Thursday afternoon in October on the corner of M Street and Georgetown Drive in Georgetown, was an empty lot.

Not a vacant building. Not a condemned structure awaiting demolition. A lot — cleared, fenced, the brick foundations of whatever had stood there last still visible at the perimeter like the outline of a memory, the ground hadn't finished releasing. A construction sign was bolted to the chain-link fence with the provisional confidence of something that had been there long enough to stop looking provisional. The sign named a developer whose name Tamara recognized and whose financial situation Rafi had mentioned, six months earlier, in a context she now found freshly relevant.

She stopped walking.

Dianne, half a step behind, stopped beside her.

They had been in Washington for three days — a girls' trip, which was what they called it because *girls' trip* was the language of leisure and leisure was the cover, though if pressed, neither of them could have articulated precisely what they were covering or for whom. They had eaten well. They had walked the city the way women who know how to walk a city walk it — with intention disguised as wandering, covering ground that looked like pleasure and was also, for reasons neither examined too closely, reconnaissance. They had a flight home the following morning.

Tamara looked at the lot.

She looked at the brick foundations. At the chain-link fence. At the corner — the specific geometry of it, the way M Street and Wisconsin met at an angle that created a particular relationship between the building footprint and the pedestrian flow, between interior and street, between privacy and visibility. She looked at the quality of the light at this intersection at this time of day, which was the light of late afternoon in October in a city that knew how to use its hours — slanted, generous, the light that made old brick look like it had been waiting for exactly this.

She looked at all of this in approximately four seconds. Then she said: *"Dianne."* Just the name. The inflection of a woman who has found something and needs a second opinion from the only person whose opinion she trusts absolutely.

Dianne looked.

She looked the way she looked at everything — from the inside out, reading the space not for what it was but for what it wanted to become. The foundations. The corner. The light. The specific relationship between the lot and the street and the pedestrian who would arrive here in the evening, after a day of doing whatever Washington asked of them, and need — without knowing they needed it — a room that understood them before they walked in.

She thought about round tables.

She thought about music calibrated to the decibel of privacy.

She thought about a corner booth and the kind of room that required one.

She thought, though she did not know why and did not pursue the question, about a kitchen in New Orleans and a transistor radio and a song that felt like hers. The thought arrived and departed like something that had been waiting at the edge of a room, uncertain of its welcome.

She was quiet for a long time.

"How much do you have left from the settlement?" she said finally.

Tamara had been waiting for this question — not this specific question, but the question that meant Dianne had seen what she'd seen. She exhaled in the way she exhaled at the top of a course when the line opened up exactly as she'd calculated it would — the exhale of commitment, of a body that has decided and a mind that has agreed and nothing left between the decision and the mountain but the doing of it.

"Enough," she said. "Rafi," Dianne said. "Obviously," Tamara said. "Seymour needs to know."

"Seymour already knows everything before we tell him. That's his whole thing."

A woman walked a small dog around them on the sidewalk with the resigned patience of someone accustomed to tourists stopping in the middle of everything for no apparent reason. She did not know she was navigating around two women in the act of making a decision that would alter, in ways that radiated outward beyond any prediction either of them could have made, a significant portion of the events of the following three years.

Nobody ever knows that. That is the nature of corners.

Dianne looked at the lot one more time.

"We always said we'd be in business together," she said.

"We said it the first time when we were nine years old," Tamara said. "In my mother's kitchen. You were eating a biscuit. You had powdered sugar on your chin, and you pointed at me and said —" she stopped.

Dianne looked at her.

The pause lasted exactly the length of a woman catching herself. Tamara had learned, across the years of this friendship that was both what it appeared to be and infinitely more, to catch herself at the edge of the before — the specific and particular before that existed in her memory and nowhere else, that she carried for both of them, that she would go on carrying until the time came when she didn't have to anymore.

She recovered in under a second.

"You said we were going to run the whole city someday," Tamara said. "My mother laughed so hard she spilled her coffee."

Dianne smiled — the warm, slightly rueful smile of a woman accustomed to the texture of a past that didn't always load when called upon. *"I don't remember that," she said.* The words carried no weight, no distress. She had made peace with the voids a long time ago.

Or she had made peace with not examining them too closely.

These were not the same thing, though she had not yet found the reason to distinguish between them.

"I know," Tamara said. "But I do."

She said it simply. The way she said everything that mattered — directly, without decoration, in the voice that lived underneath the theater.

Dianne held it for a moment. Filed it in the category she had built for exactly these moments — the things Tamara remembered that she did not, the specific and recurring evidence of a shared history she could feel but not open. The warmth of it. The weight of it. Two women on a sidewalk in Georgetown with a lifetime between them that only one of them could see.

"Call Rafi," Dianne said.

Tamara's Mountain

The injury happened on a Tuesday.

This is the detail Tamara remembered with the specific clarity of traumatic imprint — not the fall itself, not the sound that preceded the understanding of what had occurred, but the day. Tuesday. An ordinary word for an extraordinary rupture. She had been twenty-three years old, and she had been, by the assessment of coaching staffs on three continents, on the trajectory that ends with a name on a medal and a life built on the foundation of that name.

She had been pointing herself down a training course in Val d'Isère when the mountain offered its opinion.

The damage was to the knee — complex, multilayered, the kind of injury that orthopedic surgeons describe in the language of cartilage and ligament and the particular cruelty of structural failure in a system built for load — but what Tamara felt, lying in the snow in the silence that followed, was not located in the knee. It was located somewhere more central. Some load-bearing element of her sense of herself that had been, until that Tuesday, as reliable as bone.

She underwent four surgeries across eighteen months.

She did not cry at any of them, which her surgeon noted with the professional admiration of a man who had operated on many athletes and recognized the particular courage of people who have made a life from the absolute requirement of the body.

She cried once, alone, in the apartment she had rented in Lausanne during rehabilitation — a city she had chosen specifically because she knew no one in it, because the grief she needed to do required privacy. She cried with the completeness of a woman who understood that she was mourning something real and that the mourning deserved the full weight of her attention.

Then she stopped.

She had always been able to stop when she decided to. The mountain had given her that, too.

What came after was not recovery in the conventional sense — not the reassembly of a life around the absence of the thing lost — but something more architectural. She looked at what remained — the body that knew exactly where it was in space at every moment, the kinetic intelligence that had been trained to sixty miles an hour and now found its expression in the slower geometries of a dance studio floor, the fearlessness that was not recklessness but calculation, the absolute commitment to a line once chosen — and she built from it.

NYU. The theater program. The director who had told her in her second year that she was more interesting as an intelligence than as an instrument, and who had meant it as the highest compliment available in his vocabulary, which it was.

Washington. The work that came after the theater, which the theater had been preparing for in ways she had not understood until she was inside it. The work she did not discuss at dinner parties, which was the surest evidence of its importance, because Tamara discussed everything at dinner parties — everything that could be said without consequence.

Bradford Beauregard III, who had been a mistake of the specific kind that only intelligent women make — the mistake of believing that a man's capability was evidence of his character. She had been wrong about the correlation. She had spent nine years learning the precise shape of her error. She had extracted herself from it with the same quality of decision she had brought to every other course in her life — complete commitment to the line, eyes open, no looking back once the direction was chosen.

The settlement had been Bradford's attorney's recommendation and Bradford's only genuinely wise decision in the final year of their marriage. Tamara had taken it without drama, without negotiation beyond what her own attorney — a woman she had chosen specifically for the quality of her stillness in a room — had conducted on her behalf.

She had not thought of it as money.

She had thought of it as a starting gate.

She had been waiting, without knowing precisely what she was waiting for, for the course to open.

It had opened on a corner in Georgetown on a Thursday in October. She had pointed herself at it the way she had always pointed herself at the mountain — with her whole body, her whole history, her whole self — and committed to the line.

What she did not yet fully understand, standing on that sidewalk while Dianne filed the moment into one of her careful interior categories, was that this course would be different from all the others. On the mountain, the only person she could hurt by committing to the line was herself. In Georgetown, in business, in the room they were going to build together, the calculation was broader. The line ran through other people.

She understood this, at some level. She had always been good at understanding the things she was not yet ready to act on.

Dianne's Voids

She did not call them voids, privately.

She called them *lacunae* — the clinical term, the Latin word for gaps, for the spaces in a geological formation where material is absent, where you can see by the shape of the surrounding structure that something was there and is no longer. It was a precise word, and she was a precise woman, and the precision was also, she understood, a form of management — if the absence had a clinical name, it remained in the category of *known phenomena* rather than migrating into something less classifiable.

The lacunae were specific. Childhood — largely absent, available only in fragments that arrived without context or chronology, images without narrative, sensations without origin. Early education — reconstructable from records that existed, had been shown to her, and she accepted as documentary evidence of a past she could not access experientially. Relationships before a certain point — absent, with the particular completeness of a file that has not merely been misplaced but removed.

She knew, in the clinical language that was both her profession and her private vocabulary, that she had experienced a dissociative amnestic episode of significant duration and depth. She knew the neuroscience of it — the hippocampal disruption, the failure of memory consolidation under extreme trauma, the specific and sometimes permanent severance between episodic memory and the continuous narrative of self. She had written three academic papers on the subject.

She had not written about herself in any of them.

What she did not know — what lived in the largest lacuna of all, the one she had mapped most carefully and approached most obliquely — was the origin of the episode. The event. The specific and located moment at which the narrative of Dianne Montague had been interrupted.

She had a theory.

She did not examine it directly.

She had learned, from thirty years of working with trauma in other people, that the mind protected itself for reasons and that the reasons deserved respect even when the protection was no longer necessary. She had been patient with other people's silences. She extended the same patience to her own.

The restaurant was a complication she had not anticipated. She had expected the work to be external — the sourcing, the staff, the room, the music that Seymour was curating with the care of a man who understood acoustics as a form of ethics. She had not expected the restaurant itself to function as a kind of retrieval mechanism. The yellow walls she had specified for the kitchen — she had arrived at the color without deliberation, the way you arrive at the thing you've always known — and then stood in the completed space and felt the walls looking back at her with the patient expression of something that had been waiting to be recognized.

She had not said anything to anyone about the walls.

But she had noted it. Filed it in the catalog, under the growing subcategory she had labeled, with the dark precision of the forensically trained, *evidence.*

But she was a forensic neuropsychologist. Board-certified at the highest level. A woman whose professional gift was the detection of what was hidden, the understanding of why it was hidden, and the precise clinical architecture of bringing it to light.

She had noticed — recently, with increasing frequency — that the people closest to her knew something.

Not suspected. *Knew.*

She had begun to catalog the evidence the way she cataloged everything — systematically, without revealing the catalog to anyone, with the patience of a woman who understood that the most important investigations were the ones conducted in complete silence.

Tamara, who occasionally began sentences with *remember when* — stopped. Not from inattention. From the specific deliberateness of a woman editing herself in real time, which required knowing what was being edited.

Rafi, whose eyes held something when he looked at her that she had classified, provisionally, as *grief in remission.* It was not the grief of loss. It was the grief of a man who had lost something and then found it again and was still, years later, working out what to do with the finding.

Seymour, who had found her — this was the word she used, *found*, though she had never examined what it implied about her prior condition — in New Orleans, and whose certainty about her, from the very beginning, had the quality of knowledge rather than assessment. The kind of certainty that came from information, not instinct.

She was running a counter-operation on the people who loved her. She had not told any of them.

She was not ready to tell any of them. But she was getting closer.

The restaurant accelerated things, in ways she could not yet fully account for. She had expected a project. She had received, instead, a pressure system — the accumulated weight of a building and a room and a kitchen with yellow walls pressing against the underside of the thing she had been careful not to examine, pushing up through the lacunae with the quiet insistence of water finding level.

She was a precise woman. She understood what the pressure meant.

She was not yet ready to name it.

But she was, in the way of a woman who has spent a professional lifetime watching other people arrive at the same threshold, getting there.

Rafi's Notebook

The first notebook was a composition book he had bought at a drugstore in the Garden District on a Tuesday in September, the week after the towers fell, when the city was quiet in the specific way that cities go quiet when they are trying to absorb something that will not be absorbed.

He had not known, when he bought it, what it was for.

He had bought it because he needed somewhere to put things he could not say out loud, and because Rafi Delacroix — who held a doctorate in economics from the London School of Economics, who had traced money through sovereign funds and numbered accounts and the back corridors of international banking with the precision of a man who understood that money was just language and language had rules — had learned very early that the things that mattered most were the things you could not put in a report.

On the first page of the first notebook he had written a single line: *She does not remember me.*

Then he had closed the notebook and set it on his desk and sat with the fact of that sentence for a long time.

She had come back to New Orleans. That was the word Seymour had used — *come back* — though Rafi understood immediately that *come back* was not the accurate description of what had happened. A woman who had come back knew she was returning. Dianne had arrived in New Orleans the way a tide arrives: moved by something enormous and external, pulled by forces she could not have named, walking into Preservation Hall on a Friday night as though she had been sent there rather than chosen it.

Seymour had called him from outside the club at midnight. *"She's here," he had said.*

Rafi had driven from the Garden District to Frenchmen Street in eleven minutes, which was four minutes faster than the route permitted. He had stood in the doorway of Preservation Hall and looked at a woman with Dianne's face and Dianne's hands and Dianne's precise, assessing way of standing in a new room — the neuropsychologist's posture, the woman who read spaces before she spoke in them — and understood two things simultaneously.

The first: that she was alive.

He had believed she was alive. He had continued to believe it across the months when the belief required effort, when the search had produced nothing and the city she had been in that morning had stopped producing anything, when the official record had resolved its uncertainty in the only direction available to it.

But belief and knowledge were different instruments. He knew that better than anyone. And standing in the doorway of Preservation Hall at midnight, he had experienced the specific and irreplaceable shift from belief to knowledge as a physical event — something in his chest that he had been holding for five months releasing all at once, the way a hand releases something it has been gripping so long it has forgotten the grip.

The second thing: that she did not know him.

She looked at him when Seymour brought him to her table — the careful, professional assessment of a woman meeting a stranger — and Rafi saw immediately that there was no recognition. Not suppressed recognition. Not careful recognition. The clean, unpopulated look of a person who had never seen this face before.

He had introduced himself.

She had been warm and direct and curious in the way she was always warm and direct and curious, which was the detail that unmade him — that she was entirely herself and entirely absent of him simultaneously, that the woman was there and the relationship was not.

He had shaken her hand.

He had said: *It's a pleasure to meet you, Dr. Montague.*

She had said his name back to him — *Rafi Delacroix*, the way you repeat a name you want to remember, the neuropsychologist's professional habit — and he had watched the sounds of it move through her without catching on anything. No edge. No snag of the familiar. His own name, in her voice, arriving as new.

He had driven home afterward and opened the composition book and written the sentence and closed it.

She does not remember me.

He was, by the time of this novel, on his seventeenth notebook.

The notebooks were kept in a fireproof safe in his apartment two blocks from the restaurant — the safe he had specified with the same care he had brought to every other aspect of the operation, the one with the combination known only to him and, in a sealed envelope in a safety deposit box at a bank on K Street, to Tamara. The notebooks were not operational intelligence. They were not financial records. They were not, in any formal sense, anything.

They were Dianne, observed across eleven years by the person who had known her longest.

He had written down everything — every word that suggested a connection she was forming without knowing what she was connecting to, every flash of near-recognition quickly covered, every song she heard and went still at, every time she looked at a kitchen or a porch or a particular quality of afternoon light and stayed in the looking longer than the sight required.

He had written down every moment when she had almost remembered him and then not, and the specific quality of the not, and what it told him about the progress of the thing he was waiting for.

He had written, in the fourteenth notebook, on a Thursday in January: *She described a dream last week — to Tamara, who told me without knowing she was telling me. A kitchen. A radio. A song she didn't recognize but felt she knew. The kitchen has yellow walls. She's described this before. The yellow walls have been consistent across six mentions across four years. The kitchen in her mother's house on Chartres Street had yellow walls. I painted them with her the summer we were twelve. She climbed the ladder and I held it and she painted the ceiling yellow too, which her mother had not asked for, and her mother did not mind.*

I did not tell Tamara any of this. Tamara is not ready to know what the notebooks contain. She carries the before with love and with discipline, but love and discipline are not the same as readiness. There is a difference between holding a thing and being prepared to put it down.

He had written, in the sixteenth notebook, three months ago: *She has begun noticing that we know something. I can see her running her counter-operation — the catalog, the small precise questions, the way she holds a silence after one of us catches ourselves. She is good at this. She is the best I have ever seen. If she were running this investigation on anyone else it would already be closed.*

But she is running it on the people who love her. And the people who love her are good too.

It will not be much longer.

He had not written: *I am afraid of what happens when it isn't much longer.*

He had thought it. He had not written it, because Rafi Delacroix was a man who wrote things down in order to be honest with himself, and he was not yet ready to be honest with himself about that particular fear — the fear that the woman who came back from the memory would not be the woman he had spent eleven years watching come back from the memory, that something in the return would change the specific and irreplaceable thing that eleven years of proximity to her silence had built in him.

There was also the other fear. The one he had not given a sentence to in any of the seventeen notebooks, the one that lived below the economy of language he had built to manage himself. The fear that she would remember, and that the first face she would fully see again would not be his — that eleven years of patient proximity had arranged themselves on the wrong side of the thing she was returning to.

He had traced money through systems complex enough that governments paid for his analysis. He could not trace this.

He kept the notebooks.

He waited.

He sat at table four every Thursday with a glass of Meursault and a leather notebook that appeared to contain wine notes and told himself, each time, that he was waiting for the right moment.

He understood, at some level below the language he used to manage himself, that the right moment was not something he could control — that it would announce itself the way all the moments that actually mattered announced themselves, not by being ready but by being necessary.

The lot behind the restaurant he had purchased on a Tuesday.

The Tuesday after they had signed the papers on M Street and Wisconsin — the day after the LLC was registered, the business plan filed, the lease executed, the day after everything that had been a decision became a fact.

He had not told Dianne.

He had not told Tamara.

He had driven to the address of the lot — a parcel of undeveloped land behind the building's eastern wall, owned by a development company that had been planning to build and had not built and was now, quietly, willing to sell — and he had sat in his car and looked at it for a long time.

It was, at that moment, a gravel lot with a rusted fence and a view of the back of what was going to become the finest room in Georgetown.

He had seen something else. He had seen the second novel.

Not in the way that a man with a development scheme sees potential — as a financial instrument, as an abstraction waiting to be converted. In the way that a man who has spent his life loving a woman from three houses away and then from three blocks away and then from a table in her own dining room sees the space beside the thing he loves: as an inevitability. As the answer to a question that hadn't been asked yet.

He had bought it that afternoon.

He had added it to the last page of Volume Fifteen of the business plan as a footnote — a single line, in the margin, not in the body of the document: *The lot to the east belongs to the second novel. It will be ready when she is.* He had not signed the footnote.

He did not need to. He was the only person who would read Volume Fifteen's last page, and he was the only person who had bought the lot, and the only person who understood, with the full weight of an economist's training and a childhood friend's seventeen notebooks, that the most important investments were the ones that could not be valued until the moment of their use.

He had grown up, as Dianne had grown up, in a neighborhood in New Orleans that Rafi's mother had described as *close to everything and far from enough* — which was the accurate description of a neighborhood in the late 1970s and early 1980s where everyone knew each other and most people did not have quite enough and some people made the kind of decisions that proximity to not-enough produces, and where Rafi had learned, by the age of nine, that the difference between the families who stayed and the families who got out was not luck but literacy — not the literacy of reading and writing, which everyone on his street had, but the literacy of systems. Of understanding how money moved. Of reading the room before the room could define you.

He had been born with this literacy the way Freeman had been born with the music and Seymour had been born with the architecture of things. It was not a gift he had asked for or cultivated. It had simply been present, as obvious to him as color was obvious, as unmistakable as the sound of a bass string perfectly tuned.

He had read the systems. He had understood them. He had gone to London — full scholarship, the LSE, the doctorate that produced three papers that were still being cited in the field of financial forensics — and he had come back to New Orleans when his mother needed him and he had stayed because the city needed people who understood its systems and were willing to use that understanding for something other than extraction.

And because Dianne was there.

She had always been three houses down until she wasn't. Until the Tuesday in September when the world reorganized itself around the fact of towers falling and Dianne Montague was in New York and the towers fell and the search produced nothing and the city's official record resolved its uncertainty in the direction that Rafi had refused, in every private hour of the months that followed, to accept.

He had been correct not to accept it.

This was not comfort, exactly. Being right about the survival of the person you love is not the same as having them back. He had learned this at midnight in a doorway in Frenchmen Street, holding a hand that felt exactly as he remembered it and watching a face that did not know what his hands remembered.

He had kept his notebooks. He had kept the lot.

He had kept table four.

He was, in his own quiet and unannounced assessment, the most patient person in the operation. Seymour ran the room. Tamara was the room's heat. Dianne was the room's mind. Rafi was the room's memory — the man who held the full account, who had been keeping it since before the operation had a name, who would hold it until the moment it could be given back.

He looked forward to that moment the way a man looks forward to the end of a watch he chose to keep — not with impatience, which would have been an insult to what it had cost, but with the particular readiness of someone who has been standing in a doorway long enough to know exactly what kind of light comes through it when it opens.

He was not yet ready to name it. He didn't need to name it.

He knew what it was.

The Band:
Who They Really Are

Dr. Seymour Emerson did not build the house band the way other bandleaders built bands — by audition, by reputation, by the mutual recognition of musicians who had heard each other's work and wanted more of it. He built it the way he built everything: with total knowledge of what each piece needed to do and absolute patience in waiting for the right piece to arrive.

What arrived was nine people in total, which was more than a quartet and less than an orchestra and exactly right for a room calibrated to the decibel of privacy. On any given Thursday, seven of them were on the bandstand and two were elsewhere in the building doing the other work. The rotation was Seymour's to determine and he determined it with the same attention he brought to a set list — nothing arbitrary, everything intentional, the whole greater than any sum you could calculate from its parts.

What distinguished Seymour from most leaders was that he rarely evaluated people according to what they claimed they could do. He evaluated them according to what they consistently did when nobody was watching. Talent interested him. Reliability interested him more. Character interested him most of all.

The world knew them as the finest house band in Washington. The world was not wrong.

The world simply did not know everything.

The world saw musicians. Seymour saw capabilities. Dianne saw people. Between them, they had assembled something that looked entirely ordinary from the outside and became increasingly difficult to explain the longer one observed it.

Freeman Freeman

Freeman Freeman — the name was his father's gift and his father's joke simultaneously, the kind of name that announced itself before the man did and then stepped aside so the man could exceed it. He was forty-three, Louisiana-born, the product of a musical education that had begun in a Pentecostal church in Shreveport at age four and had never fully left the building even when Freeman did. The church had been small, white clapboard, and perpetually warm in summer. By the time most children were learning to sit still through a service, Freeman had already learned that music could move a room faster than a sermon. He had watched worshippers rise to their feet when a song reached the right place in their hearts, and he never forgot the lesson.

He played guitar the way certain people pray — with his whole body, with absolute conviction, with the particular fearlessness of someone who had decided early that the instrument was not a barrier between himself and the music but a direct line to it. His harmonica was something else entirely: raw, conversational, the sound of a man telling you the truth before he'd decided to.

Then there was the violin.

Most people in the dining room of Miss Dianne's Jazz and Blues Kitchen saw Freeman Freeman as a guitarist who occasionally played harmonica and sang with the effortless authority of a man born into the tradition. Which was true. What they did not see — what only appeared on certain evenings, when the set list moved into territory that called for it — was the violinist.

He had grown up with the fiddle before he grew up with the guitar. His grandfather had played Cajun music in the old way, the way it was played in the dance halls of Vermilion Parish before the highways came through and changed the geography of Saturday nights, and Freeman had learned at his knee the specific bowing style, the particular ornamentation, the way a Cajun fiddle talked to an accordion the way two old friends talk — in shorthand, in shared reference, in the music that lives between the notes.

His grandfather had never used words like technique or tradition. He had simply played, and expected the boy beside him to listen. Freeman often thought that the most important musical lessons of his life had arrived without explanation.

He could play bluegrass with the same fluency — the melodic clarity of the high lonesome style, the runs that belonged to the mountains the way his Cajun fiddle belonged to the bayou — and jazz violin in the tradition of Stéphane Grappelli, which was a different instrument entirely though it wore the same body, requiring a looseness in the wrist and a conversational quality in the bow arm that had taken him years to find and that he now deployed with the ease of a man speaking his third language.

When Freeman picked up the violin, the band became something else.

Not better. Different.

The way a river becomes different when it meets the sea — still itself, but suddenly aware of a larger context.

Guests often reacted before they understood why. Conversations softened. Heads turned. People who had been watching the room began watching the stage. The violin carried a different emotional vocabulary than the guitar, and Freeman spoke it fluently.

His voice was the room's other secret weapon.

It was a voice that had no business being as large as it was in a body as economical as his — a baritone that started somewhere below the sternum and arrived with the unhurried authority of weather. When

Freeman sang lead, the room reorganized itself around him without anyone moving.

When he sang backup, he became the thing that made whatever was in front of him sound inevitable. There was no strain in it. No visible effort. The voice simply appeared, fully formed, as though it had been waiting patiently beneath the song for the opportunity to reveal itself.

His doctorate was in organizational psychology, with a concentration in group dynamics under stress. He had written his dissertation on decision-making in closed operational units — the specific ways that small groups either held together or came apart when the pressure exceeded the design tolerance.

He kept this to himself.

Most people who met him assumed he was simply another gifted musician. Freeman encouraged the assumption. It made observation easier.

He played his guitar and his harmonica and his violin and he sang and he watched rooms the way his dissertation subjects had watched each other — with the trained attention of a man who understood that the most important information in any group was always the information nobody was saying out loud.

He noticed who interrupted whom. Who deferred. Who performed confidence and who possessed it. He noticed the split-second exchanges of eye contact that preceded decisions and the subtle shifts in posture that accompanied deception.

To most people, a dining room was a collection of tables. To Freeman, it was a living system. Alliances formed. Hierarchies emerged. Stress revealed itself. Human beings announced their intentions constantly, provided someone knew where to look.

Freeman always knew where to look.

Stephon Keyes

Stephon Keyes was thirty-nine and had the hands of a man who had spent his entire life in conversation with keyboards — broad, deliberate, the knuckles slightly enlarged in the way of pianists who had been at it since before they were old enough to reach the pedals. His mother liked to tell people that Stephon learned patterns before he learned words. Whether that was literally true depended on how strictly one defined language, but nobody who watched him play doubted the spirit of the claim.

He played piano with the formal authority of his classical training and the Hammond B3 with something entirely different: a full-bodied, full-throttle commitment that turned the instrument into a force of nature dressed as furniture. When Stephon engaged the Leslie speaker and let the Hammond breathe, the room did not so much hear it as feel it — in the chest, in the back of the knees, in the specific frequencies that bypass conscious hearing and land somewhere more fundamental.

The rotating speaker filled the room in waves rather than notes. Sound seemed to arrive from several directions at once, wrapping itself around conversations and table settings and the polished wood surfaces of the dining room until the entire space became part of the instrument.

What most people did not know — what the dining room audience never suspected when they watched his hands on the piano keys or the Hammond's manuals — was that Stephon Keyes also played the Cajun accordion. Not as a curiosity.

Not as an occasional affectation. He played it the way he played everything: with total mastery and complete conviction, the diatonic button accordion in his hands becoming something that belonged to the Louisiana soil the way cypress trees belonged to the bayou — rooted, ancient, entirely at home. The instrument carried history inside it. Weddings. Funerals. Family gatherings. Saturday-night dances in halls where generations had worn grooves into hardwood floors. Stephon understood that music was memory made audible, and he treated the accordion accordingly.

When the evening called for it, when Seymour counted off a waltz or a two-step and the room shifted from jazz to something older and more Southern and more deeply alive, Stephon set down whatever keyboard he was playing and picked up the accordion and the sound that came out of it was the sound of every dance hall from Lafayette to Lake Charles, of Saturday nights that began at dusk and ended at dawn, of music that had survived two centuries because it knew something about joy that other traditions were still working out.

Guests who had never set foot in Louisiana often found themselves smiling before they understood why. The music carried its own geography.

He and Seymour had worked out an arrangement of complementary roles with the precision of two people who respected each other completely and had no interest in competition.

Seymour was the architecture. Stephon was the weather inside it. On the songs that needed both — and Thursday nights at Miss Dianne's had more of those songs than anywhere else in the city — they found each other across the bandstand with the ease of longtime collaborators, finishing each other's harmonic sentences the way old friends finish each other's spoken ones.

There were evenings when an audience member might reasonably conclude they were improvising. They were. But what appeared spontaneous was often the product of years spent learning how the other mind worked.

His doctorate was in cryptographic mathematics from MIT. The relationship between his mathematical mind and his musical one was not incidental — he had written extensively, in classified contexts, about the structural parallels between musical composition and encryption methodology.

A melody was a code.

A chord progression was an argument. A song, properly constructed, could carry information in its architecture that no listener would recognize as information.

Patterns revealed themselves to Stephon the way landmarks revealed themselves to travelers. He saw relationships where others saw isolated events. A sequence of notes, a statistical anomaly, an encrypted transmission, a harmonic substitution — all belonged to the same family of problems.

Stephon knew this better than anyone in the building. He used it accordingly.

The fact that almost nobody realized this was one of his favorite things about the arrangement.

Dixie St. James Dixie St. James had a name that sounded like something a novelist would invent and was, in fact, exactly what her mother had written on the birth certificate in a hospital in Biloxi on a July morning thirty-seven years ago, inspired by equal parts state pride and a Fats Domino record playing in the waiting room. Dixie maintained that the story was probably exaggerated. Her mother maintained that it was not. The debate had been ongoing for thirty-seven years.

She was compact and precise and possessed of a physical stillness at the bass that belied what the instrument was doing in her hands — which was, on any given evening, holding the entire architecture of the music from underneath with the quiet authority of a foundation wall.

She played upright bass with the classical training her Tulane scholarship had given her and electric bass with the streetwise fluency of a woman who had spent her twenties on stages in New Orleans that didn't ask for your credentials before they handed you the gig. She understood groove the way structural engineers understand load — as something that either held or didn't, that either transferred correctly through the system or failed at the joint, and there was no middle ground and no partial credit.

To Dixie, rhythm was not decorative. Rhythm was infrastructure. Everything else was built on top of it.

She had a voice that she deployed like a second instrument — a rich, smoky alto that sat beneath Dianne's lead the way her bass sat beneath the band's harmonic structure: supportive, present, essential, and almost invisible until the moment it stepped forward, at which point the room understood immediately what had been holding everything up.

Like her bass playing, her singing never seemed interested in drawing attention to itself. It simply made everything around it stronger.

In rehearsal she was one of the few people willing to interrupt Seymour.

Not often.

Only when necessary.

The fact that Seymour listened when she did told newcomers everything they needed to know about her standing in the ensemble.

She had an uncommon ability to identify structural weaknesses before they became visible to everyone else.

A tempo drifting.

A transition that needed tightening.

A musical idea that sounded better in theory than in execution.

She raised objections calmly, almost gently, and was usually right.

Her doctorate was in forensic accounting from Tulane. She had worked for three years at a federal agency whose name she did not use in conversation before Seymour had found her at a session in New Orleans and offered her something more interesting.

Seymour later admitted to Dianne that he knew he was going to recruit her before the first set ended. A person capable of tracking hidden financial relationships across continents and holding perfect time through a difficult arrangement was not someone he intended to leave behind.

She had taken twenty-four hours to decide. She had not regretted it.

The forensic accounting and the bass playing turned out to have more in common than most people realized. Both involved tracing connections. Both involved finding what supported a structure and determining whether that support could be trusted.

Dixie excelled at both.

Celeste Okafor

Celeste Okafor was forty-four and played trumpet the way certain people carry themselves in a room — with the specific economy of someone who understands that what they have is sufficient and does not require announcement. She wasted neither movement nor words. People often mistook this for reserve. It was, in fact, confidence so complete it had no need to advertise itself.

She had trained at the Curtis Institute in Philadelphia, which is where the world's most serious brass players go to discover how serious the instrument truly is, and she had arrived at Curtis from Johns

Hopkins, where she had completed a doctorate in molecular biology on the protein folding mechanisms of antibiotic-resistant bacteria, which was the kind of academic combination that produced a person with very few peers and very high clearance.

At Curtis she had acquired technical mastery. At Johns Hopkins she had acquired the habit of asking questions until she reached the underlying mechanism. Together they produced a musician who rarely accepted appearances at face value.

Seymour had recruited her from a situation in Lagos that Dianne had resolved — the nature of which neither of them discussed in mixed company, and which Celeste herself referred to only as the thing in Lagos, always with the flat affect of a woman who has processed an event completely and has decided not to give it more space than it deserves.

The phrase covered a remarkable range of possibilities. Depending on who was asking, it could mean a difficult assignment, an unfortunate misunderstanding, an international incident, or all three simultaneously.

Nobody pressed for details. The handful of people who actually knew them displayed a noticeable reluctance to discuss the subject, which most observers correctly interpreted as a reason not to inquire further.

She played with precision and occasional ferocity and the specific tonal quality of a trumpeter who had also spent years studying the molecular architecture of things, which gave her an understanding of resonance — of the relationship between vibrating air columns and the physical structures through which they traveled — that was not merely musical but scientific.

Where other musicians heard sound, Celeste often heard systems. She understood how vibrations moved through materials, how frequencies reinforced or canceled one another, how architecture shaped perception.

To her, a note was never just a note. It was a physical event occurring inside a measurable environment.

She knew, better than anyone on the bandstand, exactly what the sound was doing inside the room's walls.

Long before opening night she had spent hours walking the dining room alone, producing tones at different pitches and listening to their reflections. She knew which corners accumulated resonance, which surfaces softened it, and which frequencies traveled farther than they should have.

Jerome Park had designed the surveillance kit partly with Celeste's guidance. She had told him where the frequencies lived in a dining room of this acoustic profile. He had told her what to do with them.

The resulting system was elegant beyond what either of them could have built alone.

Their collaboration possessed the particular efficiency of two experts who spoke different professional languages while describing the same phenomenon.

Jerome talked about signal pathways. Celeste talked about resonance patterns. By the third meeting they had realized they were effectively saying the same thing.

After that, progress accelerated.

Jerome Park Jerome Park was thirty-six years old and had designed every piece of surveillance equipment currently operating inside his drum kit, which meant that the most sophisticated passive intelligence collection array in any privately operated establishment in Washington, D.C. was disguised as a Gretsch Brooklyn kit in vintage satin walnut finish, which was a beautiful drum kit in addition to being everything else.

Jerome appreciated the irony. He appreciated most ironies, provided they were engineered correctly.

He had grown up in Chicago in a household where his father repaired electronics and his mother taught high school physics and the combination had produced a child who dismantled every device he was given before he understood it and reassembled it afterward better than it had been. At age nine he disassembled a clock radio to determine why it worked. At ten he modified it. At eleven he improved the reception. By twelve his parents had stopped asking where household appliances had gone and started asking when he intended to return them.

He had been doing this with increasingly complex systems ever since.

The doctorate in electrical engineering, signals and systems, from the University of Illinois had given the practice a formal vocabulary. The subsequent work — the classified work, the work done inside buildings whose addresses did not appear in public directories — had given it consequence.

He was, by the assessment of every person who had worked with him, the finest systems engineer currently operating in the field. This was a compliment he accepted without comment because he was not interested in compliments. He was interested in systems.

Systems were honest. People frequently were not. Jerome preferred honest things.

What he had built inside the kit was this: a passive audio collection array of seven directional microphones, each calibrated to a specific zone of the dining room, each feeding a signal processor the size of a hardback novel that lived inside the floor tom's false bottom. The processor ran a continuous acoustic fingerprinting algorithm that compared incoming sound against a library of vocal signatures Jerome had compiled across every evening of operation — every guest, every conversation, every frequency that had moved through the fourteen-foot ceilings of the dining room since the night they opened.

The database had begun modestly. A few dozen regulars. Several politicians. Two ambassadors. A journalist who appeared more often than his published work suggested he should have time for.

Over time it had become something else entirely.

The system did not record conversations. It did not need to record conversations.

It identified who was in the room, where they were sitting, and in some cases what emotional register the conversation was operating in — the acoustic signature of urgency, of deception, of the particular frequency pattern that Jerome had isolated and classified as operational communication, which was the language of people who were doing the same work in the same room as he was and did not know he knew.

The remarkable thing was not how often the system was correct. It was how often it detected patterns before human observers noticed them.

A recurring voice. An unusual cluster of meetings. The gradual convergence of individuals who had no apparent reason to know one another.

The Listener noticed.

The system had a name, which Jerome had given it privately and which he had not shared with anyone: The Listener.

The Listener had been running since opening night. In that time it had heard everything.

Or nearly everything. Jerome remained intellectually humble enough to acknowledge the distinction.

The system's greatest strength was not memory. It was accumulation. One conversation meant little. Fifty conversations meant something. Five hundred conversations meant a pattern.

Patterns, in Jerome's experience, were where the truth usually lived.

The Listener excelled at finding them.

The Backup Singers

This was not a formal designation.

There was no rehearsal in which Seymour had assembled Tamara and Freeman and Dixie and said: you three will back Dianne when she sings.

It had emerged the way the best things at Miss Dianne's emerged — organically, inevitably, as though the room itself had required it and the people in the room had simply responded to the requirement.

Seymour, who was ordinarily inclined toward planning, secretly trusted these developments more than the arrangements he designed himself. When something emerged naturally among gifted people, it often revealed possibilities no amount of preparation could have anticipated.

The first time it happened was at a soundcheck two weeks before opening, when Dianne was running through I'd Rather Go Blind for acoustic calibration purposes and Freeman, from across the bandstand, had quietly begun to add a harmony that fit the way a key fits a lock — with the specific, inevitable rightness of something that belonged. Dixie had come in under both of them a moment later. Tamara, who was in the dining room adjusting the placement of a table and had not been invited to this soundcheck in any musical capacity, had stopped what she was doing and walked to the edge of the stage and added the third voice as though she had always known it was hers to give.

The remarkable thing was not that she found the harmony. The remarkable thing was how quickly. There was no searching for the note, no tentative approach. She stepped into the arrangement the way a person steps into a familiar room.

Seymour had not stopped playing.

He had simply tilted his head by a fraction — the gesture of a man filing something important — and continued.

Dianne remembered that moment later with unusual clarity. The song had suddenly become larger around her. Not louder. Larger. The emotional space inside it had expanded.

After the soundcheck, nobody said anything about it. Nobody needed to.

Experienced musicians recognized certain truths immediately. This had been one of them.

On opening night, when Dianne stepped to the microphone for the first time, Tamara and Freeman and Dixie were simply there behind her — Tamara off the stage floor, Freeman on his stool with his guitar in his lap, Dixie at her bass — and the room received them as though the arrangement had always existed, which in the only way that mattered, it had.

What they gave Dianne when they sang behind her was not merely harmonic support. It was something more structural than that.

They gave her a surround — a sonic architecture that held her voice the way the room held its guests: completely, warmly, with the specific security of a space that had been built to make you feel that whatever you brought into it was safe.

Dianne sang differently with them behind her.

More openly. More completely.

As though the support allowed her to go to the places in a song she might not have gone alone.

There are moments in music when trust becomes audible. This was one of them.

The audience rarely understood exactly what they were hearing. They simply knew that something about the sound felt unusually complete.

None of the four of them had ever discussed this. All four of them knew it was true.

Some arrangements require rehearsal. Others require recognition.

This one belonged firmly to the second category.

When The Room Goes Full Dixieland

On certain evenings — unannounced, unscheduled, arriving the way weather arrives, by the accumulated pressure of a room that has reached the particular temperature that requires it — Miss Dianne's Jazz and Blues Kitchen became something larger than itself.

Regular guests learned to watch for the signs. Not because anyone announced them, but because patterns eventually reveal themselves.

It began always the same way: Seymour's left hand finding a riff that was older than jazz, older than blues, rooted in the streets of New Orleans before the music had a name for what it was. Freeman reaching for the violin instead of the guitar. Stephon setting down the accordion and pulling the Hammond's full register up from where he'd been keeping it in reserve. A subtle shift would pass through the room. People who had been focused on conversations began paying attention to the stage. Longtime patrons exchanged knowing looks.

And then — from the service corridor, from the kitchen pass, from whatever corner of the dining room they happened to be occupying in their professional capacity at that moment — three members of the wait staff who were not merely wait staff.

They had been hired that way.

This had been Seymour's condition, stated once, at the first meeting about staffing, in a manner that made clear it was not a suggestion: Three of the floor staff play brass. I need trumpet, trombone, and saxophone with clarinet capability. They serve dinner until I need them. When I need them, they put down the tray.

Dianne had looked at him across the round table in the war room. "Can they wait tables?" she had asked.

"Exceptionally," Seymour had said. "Can they keep a secret?" "They already are."

She had approved the condition.

Years later she would occasionally wonder whether that conversation should have prompted more questions than it had.

Then she would remember the music and decide it had worked out exactly as intended.

Their names, on the staff roster that the restaurant's HR documentation showed any interested party: Marcus Tureaud, senior server, eleven years in fine dining, references impeccable. Solange Arceneaux, server and sommelier assistant, formerly of two Michelin-starred establishments in New Orleans and Chicago. Roy Baptiste, floor manager on Thursday evenings, known among the regular guests for remembering their preferred tables, their wine preferences, and their birthdays.

Their names, in the other context: the same. These were not cover identities. These were real people with real skills in both directions, which was the only kind Seymour accepted.

He had long ago concluded that the best disguises were not disguises at all.

Marcus Tureaud played trumpet with the brassy authority of a man who had come up in the second line tradition of New Orleans — the street-level, parade-born, swinging-from-the-shoulder style of trumpet playing that had originated in the funerals and the celebrations and the long walk between them that New Orleans had always understood were the same journey. He was thirty-five and he moved through a dining room with the grace of someone equally comfortable on a parade route.

Even carrying a tray, he projected the loose confidence of a man who expected music to break out at any moment.

Solange Arceneaux played trombone. She had the physical ease with the slide that only comes from having started young, the instrument becoming an extension of the arm rather than an appendage attached to it. Her tone was warm in the low register and bright at the top and she could play tailgate — the old, raw, wide-open Dixieland trombone style — with the conviction of a woman who understood that some musical traditions were not historical artifacts but living things that needed people to keep them breathing.

There was joy in her playing that resisted analysis. Audiences responded to it immediately.

Roy Baptiste played saxophone and clarinet with the double-instrument fluency that the Dixieland tradition had always demanded of its reed players. His clarinet in the upper register was the sound of the style — the weaving, obligato line that danced above the ensemble the way starlings move above a field: individually free, collectively shaped, the whole more beautiful than any single part could account for.

His tenor saxophone was something earthier, something that belonged more to the blues than to the parade, and he moved between the two instruments the way certain people move between languages — without thinking about it, which is the only way it works.

Watching him switch instruments felt less like a change and more like a translation.

When Seymour's left hand found the riff and the signal went out through the room — not a spoken signal, never a spoken signal, simply the music itself modulating into the register that meant it is time — Marcus Tureaud set down his tray with the care of a man who had been waiting for this moment without showing that he'd been waiting, and picked up the trumpet that had been resting, throughout the evening, in a specific location that appeared to any casual observer as a staging area for service equipment.

Solange Arceneaux retrieved her trombone from behind the service bar where it had leaned against the wall behind a curtain since before the first guest arrived, wrapped in a cloth that looked like a table linen until it didn't.

Roy Baptiste opened the case that had been beneath the host stand since seven o'clock, beneath a tablecloth that had been draped there for the purpose, and assembled his clarinet in the time it took Stephon to play a single sixteen-bar chorus.

They took the stage.

The audience invariably loved this part. The transformation happened quickly enough to feel magical and naturally enough to feel inevitable.

And Miss Dianne's Jazz and Blues Kitchen — which had been, moments before, the finest intimate jazz room in Georgetown — became a full Dixieland band in the tradition of the city that had invented it.

Seven on the bandstand. The ensemble sound filling the room from the floor to the fourteen-foot ceilings to the original plasterwork that had heard a great many things in its life and now heard this.

The room did not merely become louder. It became larger.

The music occupied every available inch of space and somehow still felt welcoming.

The guests who were present on the evenings when it happened told the story for months afterward.

They could not explain precisely what made it so extraordinary — the music, yes, the surprise of it, yes, but also something else, something in the way the room received it, something in the quality of collective joy that a full Dixieland ensemble produces in an enclosed space when every player is exactly where they are supposed to be.

People brought friends back hoping to witness it again. Some succeeded. Others did not. The unpredictability only increased the legend.

What they were responding to, though they had no way of knowing it, was the feeling of a group of people who trusted each other completely performing at the outer limit of their shared capability.

There is no sound in the world quite like it. Miss Dianne's had it in abundance.

The versatility of the band was, in its operational dimension, its greatest security feature. A jazz quartet was a jazz quartet. A seven-piece Dixieland ensemble was a parade. A small group playing Cajun waltz with accordion and violin was a dance hall transported north. And the transitions between these configurations — the fluid, natural, utterly unforced movement from one sound world to another — made the bandstand a moving target that no surveillance architecture designed for a static environment could fully map.

The room was never precisely the same room twice. That was the point.

Microphone placement depended upon assumptions. Visual surveillance depended upon patterns. Predictive analysis depended upon repetition. Seymour had designed an environment that offered none of those things for very long.

Seymour understood this from the beginning.

He understood that people paid attention selectively. Most observers noticed the music and stopped there. The exceptional observers noticed the personnel changes. Almost nobody noticed the way the two interacted.

Jerome understood it from the moment he designed the kit.

From a systems perspective, variability was protection. The more fluid the environment became, the more difficult it was to establish a reliable baseline. Without a baseline, anomalies became harder to identify.

Stephon understood it the day he first set the Cajun accordion beside the Hammond B3 and watched Dianne's eyes when she saw both instruments together and understood what they implied about the range of possibility.

What looked like artistic flexibility was, in practical terms, operational flexibility. One configuration attracted one audience. Another attracted a different audience. Together they produced a clientele so varied that no outsider could easily determine who belonged and who did not.

Freeman understood it the way he understood most things — not as a theory but as a lived fact, as obvious as the grain in a piece of wood, as unremarkable to him as breathing.

Human beings revealed themselves differently in different environments. Change the music and you changed the emotional temperature of the room. Change the emotional temperature and people told different stories.

The band was the room.

The room was the operation.

The distinction between those two realities had become increasingly theoretical over time.

What began as a restaurant with extraordinary musicians had evolved into something more integrated than any of them had originally anticipated. The music informed the operation. The operation protected the music. Each strengthened the other until separating them no longer made practical sense.

And on the evenings when Marcus Tureaud reached for his trumpet and Solange Arceneaux unwrapped her trombone and Roy Baptiste assembled his clarinet and Freeman drew his bow across the violin strings and Stephon reached not for the Hammond but for the accordion and Seymour's hands found the oldest riff in the city's memory — the operation was at its most beautiful.

Everything that made the enterprise function became visible at once. Trust. Discipline. Timing. Experience. Loyalty. The rare chemistry that cannot be manufactured and can only be earned over time.

The guests saw a band.

The band saw one another.

And beneath both realities, unseen by almost everyone present, another layer of activity continued quietly and efficiently, moving to the same rhythm as the music itself.

And therefore, at its most dangerous.

Because beauty attracts attention.

Because joy lowers defenses.

Because people reveal more of themselves when they believe they are simply enjoying an evening among friends.

Seymour knew this. Dianne knew it. Jerome, Celeste, Freeman, Stephon, Dixie, Marcus, Solange, and Roy knew it too.

The greatest concealment is often not darkness but illumination — giving people something so genuine, so engaging, so unquestionably real that they never think to look beyond it.

The band was real.

The music was real.

The joy was real.

That was what made the arrangement work.

Nothing about it was a performance except the performance itself.

And therefore, at its most dangerous.

Chapter One:
Poinciana

For nine months, the band had been good.

This was Seymour's private problem. He did not name it because he did not need to name it — he was the only person inside it, and inside it the diagnosis was as obvious as a bone out of socket.

The band had been good.

Good was not the problem in theory. Good was what you aimed for on the first Thursday and the second Thursday and the third Thursday of a new room, in a new city, with musicians who were extraordinary individually and who had not yet discovered what they were collectively. Good was the inevitable condition of a band finding its way to something larger than good. Good was the waiting room.

Nine months was too long to be in the waiting room.

The length of it bothered him more than he admitted. Not to the band. Not to Dianne. Possibly not even to himself. But nine months was long enough for a room to reveal its nature, and this room was still withholding something.

Seymour had built rooms before. He had built them in New Orleans and Chicago and once, memorably and briefly, in a basement club in London that had lasted six weeks before the landlord discovered what the back room was also being used for. He understood the metabolism of a new room — the way the first weeks were raw and oversized, the way the middle months settled into a competence that could calcify into habit if the bandleader did not catch it. He had caught it in every room he had ever built.

He had not caught it here.

The problem was not the musicians. The musicians were the finest group of individual players he had ever assembled, and he had assembled groups in cities that took their music seriously. Jerome Park at the drums was a precision instrument in human form. Stephon Keyes on the Hammond and piano understood harmonic architecture the way structural engineers understood load. Dixie St. James on the bass held the floor with the unhurried authority of someone who understood that the bass line was not the rhythm section's contribution to the music but the music's foundation, and that a foundation did not announce itself. Celeste Okafor on trumpet played with an economy that other trumpeters spent careers trying to learn and most never did.

And Freeman.

Freeman Coulter Freeman, on guitar and harmonica and, on the evenings when the room asked for it, the violin — Freeman was the room's other secret weapon, the one that appeared when least expected and landed hardest because it had not been telegraphed. His voice was a baritone that started somewhere below the sternum and arrived with the unhurried authority of weather. When Freeman sang lead, the room reorganized itself around him without anyone moving.

Seymour had seen it happen often enough that it no longer surprised him. It still impressed him. There were singers who commanded attention and singers who earned it. Freeman somehow did both at the same time.

The band was extraordinary.

And for nine months it had been playing extraordinarily well.

And for nine months Seymour had been waiting for the band to stop playing well and start playing true.

These were not the same thing. The distinction was difficult to explain and impossible to quantify. Seymour had spent most of his life pursuing it anyway.

He had known this since he was six years old and his grandfather had played him a record on a Sunday afternoon in New Orleans that had reorganized the geography of his interior life, and he had been pursuing the difference between them ever since.The conversation happened on a Tuesday.

Not a service night. A Tuesday in the ninth month, in the basement rehearsal room that Seymour used for the kind of thinking that required a piano and an audience of one. He had called the full band down — which was unusual, because Seymour did not call full-band meetings unless the information required everyone to receive it simultaneously.

That fact alone had gotten everyone's attention. Seymour was not a man given to unnecessary meetings. If he called one, there was a reason.

They sat around the rehearsal room in the particular arrangement of musicians who are not playing: Jerome on an equipment case, arms crossed, waiting with the patience of a man who had learned that waiting was also a precision skill. Stephon at the upright on the far wall, his hands in his lap, still. Dixie on a folding chair with her bass between her knees, one finger idling on the E string without touching it enough to produce a note. Celeste standing at the back wall, trumpet case at her feet. Marcus Tureaud, Solange Arceneaux, and Roy Baptiste — the three who served dinner until the music needed them — arranged near the door in the posture of people who understood that the meeting was about something they already half knew.

Dianne was upstairs, which was where Dianne was when the operational dimension was not immediately required. The meeting was not operational. Tamara was at the bar, which was where Tamara was when she was listening to something she did not want to appear to be listening to, which was often.

Tamara would have denied she was listening if asked. Nobody would have believed her.

Seymour stood at the piano. He did not play.

"Nine months," he said.

He said it the way he said things that required no elaboration — without inflection, as a statement of fact that contained its own commentary. "Nine months," he said again. "We have been in this room for nine months and we are very good and we have not yet found the thing. You all know what I mean. I am not going to explain what I mean."

Nobody asked him to explain. Jerome uncrossed his arms.

Around the room there were small shifts of posture, the kind that happen when people hear something they already know but have not yet heard spoken aloud.

"So," Seymour said. "What's the card. Who has it. Someone has it. In nine months of sitting inside this problem I have come to believe that someone in this room has been holding the card and has not yet played it."

The rehearsal room was quiet.

Not an uncomfortable silence. A searching one.

Then Freeman reached into his shirt pocket.

He did not pull out the harmonica. He pulled out nothing — the gesture of reaching into his pocket was the gesture of a man reaching for the instrument of thought, the physical tic of someone who processed through the hands. He had nothing in his pocket. He turned the nothing in his fingers for a moment.

"Ahmad Jamal," he said. "Poinciana. The 1958 recording. The one with Vernel Fournier at the drums."

The room waited.

Freeman had everyone's attention now. That was not unusual. The reason for it was.

"Vernel was a New Orleans drummer," Freeman said. "People forget that. They hear the sophistication of the Ahmad Jamal Trio and they think Chicago. They think the Pershing. They think the Arie Crown. They don't think New Orleans. But Vernel was from New Orleans and what Vernel played on that record is the second line in patent leather shoes. One hundred and thirty bpm, not a click faster. The brushed groove on the ride cymbal that is the most patient and most devastating thing a drummer has done to that tempo."

He stopped.

He looked at the room.

"I have always believed," Freeman said, "that there was a Dixieland version of Ahmad's arrangement waiting inside that record. Not a cover. Not an homage. A version that takes what Vernel built and does what Vernel's New Orleans blood was pointing toward without knowing it. You take the groove and you keep it. Exactly. You take Israel Crosby's bass figure — Dixie, you know the one — and you keep it. You keep Ahmad's space. The bars where he doesn't play. The silence that is the point of the song. You keep all of it." As he spoke, the arrangement seemed to become more real simply by being described.

"And then," Stephon said.

"And then," Freeman said, "you bring in the horns. Trumpet with a Harmon mute. Trombone with a plunger. Clarinet open above everything, finding the line that Ahmad's right hand was always reaching toward without ever arriving."

He paused.

"Not Al Hirt," he said. "Not Pete Fountain. The ghosts of Al Hirt and Pete Fountain. The way they would have played it if they had heard Ahmad's record on a Tuesday afternoon at the Famous Door and gone back to the club that night and tried to find what was inside it. The way their ghosts play it in the room at two in the morning when nobody is listening."

The rehearsal room held this.

The image landed because every musician in the room understood exactly what he meant.

"That's the card," Marcus Tureaud said. He was not asking. "That's the card," Solange said.

"That's the card," Roy said, quietly, the way Roy said the things he meant. Seymour looked at Freeman.

"Freeman," he said. "Yes."

"Why have you not played me this idea before today." Freeman considered.

"Because the room hadn't asked for it yet," he said. "And because I hadn't been asked."

Nobody smiled, but several people looked down. It was exactly the sort of answer Freeman would give.

He turned the nothing in his fingers one more time.

"You asked," he said.

Seymour looked around the room. He had played enough first-read sessions in his life to know what a band's face looked like when it had heard the right answer.

This was the face.

Not excitement. Recognition.

"All right," Seymour said. "We have a chart to write."

They wrote it standing up.

Not sitting. Not at the piano. Seymour at the whiteboard and Freeman at his elbow and Jerome at the drum kit running figures as they discussed them, the arrangement emerging from the conversation the way the best arrangements emerged — from the argument between what the musicians heard in their heads and what the instruments said when asked.

Nobody seemed particularly interested in ownership. The arrangement belonged to whoever could hear the next piece of it.

The tempo was confirmed at one hundred and twenty-eight beats per minute. Not Jamal's one thirty-two. Four clicks slower, because the room was longer than the Pershing and the reverb would eat four clicks if they were not accounted for.

Jerome worked out Vernel's figure on the hi-hat — the whisper-brush pattern that was the heartbeat of the original — and adapted it for the brushed snare the arrangement required. He played it sixteen bars while the rest of the band listened. He played it the way Vernel had played it: as though he had all the time in the world and had decided to spend it exactly here.

Dixie found Israel Crosby's bass line in the second bar of Jerome's demonstration and came in underneath without discussion. Her upright walked the figure in the low register with the patient authority of a woman who understood that a bass line was not decoration but infrastructure, and that infrastructure did not announce itself.

The groove arrived almost immediately. Not finished, but recognizable.

Freeman played the melody through once on guitar — clean, unhurried, Ahmad's own voicing as close as a guitar could render it. The melody of Poinciana was not a complicated melody. Its genius was in its patience. It waited. It returned. It did not try to be more than it was, which was the reason it could become anything.

Then Marcus Tureaud picked up his trumpet.

He fitted the Harmon mute into the bell. He had three Harmon mutes — one with the stem in, one with the stem removed, one he had modified himself with a piece of electrical tape that changed the resonance in a way no manufacturer had intended and that produced a sound that lived somewhere between Miles Davis and a question asked in a dark room. He used the modified one.

He played the melody once.

The sound that came out of the modified Harmon was the sound that Freeman had described — the ghost of Al Hirt, the ghost of the Famous Door, the ghost of what New Orleans brass would have done with Ahmad's patience if it had ever thought to try.

The rehearsal room went very quiet. "Yes," Seymour said.

Just that.

No one argued for a different direction after that.

Solange Arceneaux fitted the plunger mute to her trombone — not the orchestral plunger, the one she had brought from New Orleans, the one her teacher had given her that was older than her career and had been played in every room the city had to offer. She found the counter-melody under Marcus's line and the two horns spoke to each other in the language that brass had been developing since the parade routes of the 1890s, the language of call and response and elaboration and the return.

Roy Baptiste assembled his clarinet.

He did not use a mute. The clarinet needed no mute because the clarinet in the high register was itself a kind of openness — above the conversation, above the argument, finding the line that connected everything below it the way a clothesline connects two houses. His clarinet above Solange's plunger trombone above Marcus's Harmon trumpet was three colors in a palette that had not existed until this Tuesday afternoon in a basement in Georgetown.

Stephon found the chord on the Hammond.

He used the lowest register of the B3 — the place where the Hammond stopped sounding like a keyboard instrument and started sounding like the ground itself, like the specific vibration of the earth beneath a city that knows how to move. The Leslie turned slowly. He did not engage the fast rotation. This arrangement did not need the Leslie to hurry. This arrangement needed the Leslie to breathe.

The room seemed to lean toward the sound.

They ran it twice.

The first time through was the arrangement finding its own edges — the places where something needed to open up and the places where something needed to land. The second time through was the arrangement understanding what it was.

By the middle of the second pass, they were no longer discussing possibilities. They were confirming them.

By the end of the second pass the room was doing what Seymour had been waiting nine months for the room to do.

The room was not good. The room was true.

The Thursday came three weeks later.

Seymour had not told anyone the arrangement was coming. Not Dianne. Not Tamara. Not Rafi, who sat at table four with his Meursault and his notebooks and his financial surveillance and his other thing — the patient, private other thing that Seymour understood and did not name because naming it was not his to do. He had told no one.

Some things improved when announced. Others improved when discovered. Seymour believed this arrangement belonged firmly in the second category.

The room did not need to be told. The room would know when it arrived. The evening ran its first two hours in the architecture it had built across nine months — Seymour's standard opening, the Georgetown standards, the specific calibration of music and room temperature that had made Miss Dianne's Jazz and Blues Kitchen what it was. Good. Precise. Warm. The room it had always been.

At nine forty-seven, between the second and third song of the second set, Seymour let a silence fall.

It was not a performing silence. It was not the silence he built between songs when he was managing the room's temperature. It was the silence of a man arriving somewhere he had been traveling toward for a long time.

A few regulars noticed it immediately. Most simply felt it.

He looked at Jerome.

Jerome's right hand found the hi-hat.

The brushed whisper of Vernel Fournier's figure began — patient, exact, one hundred and twenty-eight beats per minute, the heartbeat of a different song in a different time dressed in the clothes of this room on this Thursday in October.

The dining room did not react immediately.

This was correct. The arrangement did not ask for an immediate reaction. The arrangement asked for a minute of listening before the listening understood what it was listening to. Vernel's figure on Jerome's hi-hat was the invitation — understated, unhurried, the invitation that only revealed itself as an invitation when you were already inside it. Dixie came in at bar five.

She walked Israel Crosby's bass line in the low register of her upright with the patience of a woman who understood that the bass line was the argument the rest of the music was having with the ground. The dining room felt it before it heard it — in the sternum, in the back of the knees, in the specific frequency that bypassed conscious hearing and landed somewhere more fundamental.

A few guests shifted in their chairs without knowing why. The body often recognizes a groove before the mind catches up.

Freeman played the melody through once on guitar.

Clean. Unhurried. Ahmad's voicing. The melody of Poinciana arriving in a Georgetown dining room the way it had arrived at the Pershing in Chicago in 1958 — as though it had always been there and was only now being noticed.

Then Marcus Tureaud set down his tray.

He set it down on the service shelf with the care of a man who understood that the tray was not the important thing and that the important thing was already in his hand — the trumpet, the modified Harmon mute fitted into the bell, the instrument of the ghost of Al Hirt standing at the Famous Door on a Tuesday night that had never happened but was happening now.

The sound he made was the sound Freeman had described in the rehearsal room.

The dining room heard it.

Not the sound of a trumpet playing well. The sound of a trumpet playing true — the specific and irreversible difference between competence and the thing that competence was always reaching toward. The modified Harmon in the bell of Marcus's trumpet in the acoustic space of a room built for exactly this frequency was a sound the room recognized without knowing it had been waiting for it.

Rafi looked up from his notebook. He did not stop writing immediately. Then he realized he had stopped writing three measures ago.

Conversations stopped.

Not all at once. The way conversations stop when a room has shifted and the people in the room have not consciously registered the shift but their bodies have — a gradual lowering of voices, a turning of heads, the specific quality of forty occupied people becoming forty attending people.

Solange Arceneaux retrieved her trombone from behind the service bar. The plunger mute engaged. She found the counter-melody — the ghost of Pete Fountain's ghost, the brass conversation that New Orleans had been having with itself since before the parade routes had names. The plunger and the Harmon spoke to each other across the bandstand in the language that Freeman had heard in the Famous Door that had never existed, the language that was now existing for the first time in this room.

Roy Baptiste assembled his clarinet at the host stand.

In the time it took Stephon to play one sixteen-bar chord on the Hammond — the low register, the Leslie turning slowly, the ground beneath the conversation — Roy had the clarinet assembled and was finding the line above the horns, the open high register, the thread that connected everything below it.

The three of them walked to the stage.

Together. Without hurry. The way you walk toward something you have been practicing toward for months without knowing what you were practicing for. They took their positions.

No announcement accompanied the movement. None was necessary. The music itself had become the announcement.

And the room — which had been, moments before, the finest intimate jazz room in Georgetown on a Thursday evening in October — became something it had not been before and would not forget being.

The groove settled.

Not the groove of a band playing together. The groove of a band that had found the specific frequency at which eight people and one room understood each other completely. Jerome's hi-hat whispered the second line in patent leather shoes. Dixie's bass walked the figure with the patience of a woman who had been waiting nine months to walk this particular line in this particular room. Freeman's guitar held the melody at the center. The three horns braided above and around it — the Harmon's question, the plunger's answer, the clarinet's long open line above the argument.

Stephon's Hammond breathed beneath all of it. The Leslie turned.

The room held its breath. Dianne came out of the kitchen. She had been upstairs in her office — the third floor office that was not on any floor plan, the room where she did the work that could not be done in the dining room — when the first note of Jerome's hi-hat figure reached her through the floor. She had set down her pen. She had listened. She had let two full bars pass before she moved.

By the fourth bar she already knew something unusual was happening downstairs. By the eighth she was on her feet.

She came down the back stairs. She came through the kitchen.

She stood in the service corridor entrance and looked at her room. Her room.

It was doing what she had built it to do. Not what she had intended — she had not intended this specifically, had not known this was what the room was capable of — but what the room had been oriented toward from the first moment she had stood on the corner of M and Wisconsin and looked at an empty lot and understood, without knowing why, that this corner was the room she had been building toward her whole life.

The forty-two guests in the dining room had stopped performing the activity of having dinner.

They were simply present. Present in the way that people become present when something true is happening in the same room as they are — without effort, without decision, without the social performance of attention. They were there because the room had taken them there and they had not had the option of resistance.

Dianne had seen good rooms do this before. She had never seen one do it quite this completely.

Dianne watched the bandstand.

She watched Marcus Tureaud's bell and the ghost inside it.

She watched Solange's plunger moving in the conversation that was also a remembering.

She watched Roy's clarinet finding the line that connected everything. She watched Seymour's hands — at the piano now, he had moved from the Hammond to the piano at bar thirty-two with the unhurried certainty of a man who had known this moment was coming and had spent the time between then and now preparing to be inside it — his left hand walking the bass figure, his right hand finding the specific voicing that made the piano sound like it was asking the question the horns were answering.

She had spent months watching this band become a band. This was the first time she had watched it become something else.

She watched Freeman.

Freeman had put down the guitar. He had opened the violin case.

He drew the bow across the strings once — a long open note, clear and unhurried — and then found the counter-melody above Roy's clarinet, the voice above the voice above the conversation, the place where the arrangement had been incomplete without knowing it and was now complete.

The Cajun fiddle in the upper register above a Dixieland horn arrangement above a piano voicing that Ahmad Jamal had built in Chicago in 1958 was a sound that had not existed before this moment.

It was the sound of the room.

Not the room as architecture. Not the room as a business. The room as an idea finally discovering its own voice.

Dianne stood in the service corridor entrance and let it arrive.

She thought: this is what I was building toward. She thought: I did not know it was this.

She thought: but it is this. She walked to the bar.

She stood at the bar with her hands flat on the bar top and watched her room find the thing it had been waiting nine months to find.

Tamara was already at the bar.

She had come in from the front before the arrangement was two minutes old, because Tamara's kinetic intelligence — the intelligence that had read terrain at sixty miles an hour and now read rooms — had registered the shift in the room's atmosphere from the corner booth and brought her to the bar the way a compass needle is brought to north.

She stood beside Dianne. They did not speak.

They watched.

Neither woman felt any need to explain what they were hearing. The music was doing an adequate job of explaining itself.

The groove continued. The arrangement did not build toward a climax — it was not that kind of music, not the music of escalation and release. It was the music of deepening. Each pass through the chord changes took the room somewhere it had not been on the previous pass, not higher but further in, the way certain rivers take you not toward the sea but toward the source.

At the third chorus Marcus opened his bell.

He removed the Harmon mute — a single smooth motion, no interruption to the phrase, the mute in his hand and the open bell suddenly filling the room with the full sound of a trumpet in a space that had been calibrated for exactly this trumpet in exactly this acoustic. The ghost departed. What remained was not a ghost but a man — Marcus Tureaud, thirty-five years old, from New Orleans, who had grown up in the second-line tradition and was now playing that tradition in the finest intimate room in Georgetown for forty-two people who had come for dinner and were receiving something else.

The open bell was like a door opening. The room went with it.

Several people smiled without realizing they had done so.

Solange removed her plunger. Roy's clarinet climbed a register.

Freeman's bow found the top of the fiddle's range and stayed there, the sound of the high lonesome tradition of a man from Shreveport who had learned Cajun music before he learned anything else and never lost the thread back to either room.

Jerome opened the hi-hat.

Dixie's bass walked faster — not rushing, not breaking the tempo, but alive inside it in a way it had not been alive before, the instrument and the woman both fully present in the groove the way a river is fully present in its own current.

The Leslie engaged the fast rotation.

The Hammond breathed out.

The sound that filled the room was the sound of a band that had found the specific frequency at which eight musicians and one room became something none of them were individually — the seventh and final and most important thing, the thing that could not be planned or rehearsed toward but only arrived in the moment when every element was present and every element was true.

It lasted only a few minutes. Most transformations do. The fact that they are temporary is part of what makes them valuable.

The room erupted.

Not with applause — applause would come later, the specific and earned applause of a room that understood what it had witnessed. What erupted first was something that had no name and needed none: the sound of forty-two people deciding simultaneously and without discussion that they were no longer able to contain what the music was doing to them.

The former ambassador at table six stood up.

The woman at table eleven who had been in Washington for forty years and had eaten in every serious room the city had ever offered and had never once left her table before the check arrived left her table.

Three separate conversations at three separate tables stopped mid-sentence and did not resume.

Nobody seemed embarrassed by any of it. The room had moved beyond self-consciousness.

The arrangement resolved.

Seymour's hands came off the keys. Jerome lifted the brushes from the hi-hat. The bass note found its own ending. Freeman drew the bow across the strings in one long diminuendo — not stopping, tapering, the way a river tapers to stillness in a pool that has no outlet.

The room sat in what remained.

Then the applause came. The specific applause of a room that has received something it did not have words for — beginning in several places simultaneously, building not by contagion but by recognition, by the communal understanding that what had just happened deserved more than silence but that silence was the more honest response and that the applause was the compromise between honesty and gratitude.

Freeman set down his violin.

He pressed his right hand briefly to his chest — the gesture of a man from a Pentecostal church in Shreveport who had learned before he learned anything else that music of this kind required gratitude before it required anything else.

Seymour looked at his band. His band looked back.

No one smiled immediately. They were still inside the music.

"Yes," Seymour said. "That is the room."

Outside, on the corner of M Street and Wisconsin, a man in a dark coat stopped walking.

He had been passing the building on his way somewhere else. He was always on his way somewhere else. He had been in Washington for eleven months and in that time he had been on his way somewhere else in every waking hour, because the work required it and the work was everything. He stopped.

He looked at the building.

Through the brick and the Federal-period windows and the specific acoustic properties of a building that had been holding music in its walls since before the music had a name for what it was — through all of this — he heard something.

Not the melody. Not the arrangement. Something underneath those things. Something that made him pause when he ordinarily did not pause.

He could not have said what he heard. He was not a musical man, not in the way that the people inside the building were musical. But he heard something that had no category in his operational vocabulary and that required him to stop walking and stand on the sidewalk in the October cold and listen.

He stood there for the duration of the applause. Then he walked on.

He did not look back.

The fact that he did not look back would matter later. Men like him rarely looked back. They preferred to return.

He would come back in three weeks.

He would not know, when he came back, that the room he was walking into had found itself on this Thursday night, in this arrangement, in the thirty-two bars of Poinciana that had been waiting inside Ahmad Jamal's 1958 recording for sixty-six years for someone to play them this way.

He would only know that the room felt, from the moment he entered it, like somewhere he had been before.

He had not been there before.

But the room had been waiting for him.

The room had been waiting for everyone who would come through its door. It had been holding its music since 1887.

It knew how.

Below the dining room, in the war room twelve steps down, the photograph sat in the center of the round table in the dark.

Two girls on a porch in New Orleans. One pointing.

One laughing.

The photograph had occupied that position long enough that it had become part of the room's geography. People stopped noticing it only after they had noticed it completely.

The last note of Poinciana had found its way through the floor and into the room below and had hung in the air above the photograph for a moment before the building absorbed it.

The amber light burned steady. The tunnel waited.

It always waited. Patiently. Without complaint. Like the building itself.

Outside on the corner of M and Wisconsin, October moved through the city the way October always moved through Washington — with the particular authority of a season that knows its time is short and means to be felt.

The building stood at the corner and held its light. It had been holding light since 1887.

It knew how.

End of Chapter One

Interlude: The Anomaly

Jerome Park — Three Weeks Before the Thursday of Chapter Two
He saw it on a Wednesday.

Not the first Wednesday. The third Wednesday of the third month of operation, which was also the forty-first evening of service and the twenty-second Thursday he had run the array from inside the kit, and which was, by any operational measure, a night like the others — the room full, the music right, Selin at table seven beginning the pattern of appearances that Dianne had been tracking and Jerome had been cataloguing in parallel from a different angle.

He saw it at eleven forty-seven, which was after Dianne had concluded the third song and the room was settling and he was running the standard close-of-service diagnostic on the array, the way a pilot runs a post-flight checklist — methodically, without expectation of finding anything, because the expectation of finding nothing was precisely what made you find something when it was there.

It was there.

A single anomalous signature in the signal processor's acoustic log — a frequency pattern that did not belong to any voice he had catalogued, that did not belong to any instrument on the bandstand, that did not belong to the building's HVAC cycle or the street noise from M and Wisconsin or any of the forty-seven baseline frequencies he had mapped in the first two weeks of operation and logged as ambient.

The anomaly was brief. Eleven-tenths of a second. The duration of a breath. Long enough to register. Short enough to dismiss, if he had been anyone else.

He almost missed it.

He filed it and said nothing.

Jerome trusted curiosity. He trusted verification more.

He came back the next morning at six.

The building was empty at six in the morning except for Antoine, who arrived at five-thirty to begin prep and who acknowledged Jerome's presence with the nod of a man who had learned, across the months of this operation, that people arrived at unusual hours for reasons he did not need and did not want to know. Jerome appreciated this about Antoine. Antoine understood the boundaries of his lane with a precision that most people with doctorates could not match.

Jerome sat at the kit and opened the processor's archive.

The archive ran from opening night to the close of last evening's service — forty-one evenings, six hundred and some hours of acoustic data, compressed and indexed and searchable by frequency signature, by time code, by seat location in the dining room, by vocal register.

He ran a search for the anomalous frequency. He expected one result.

He found nineteen.

Jerome stared at the number for a moment. One result would have been explainable. Nineteen suggested a pattern.

The nineteen instances were distributed across the full forty-one evenings of operation. Not every evening — eleven of the forty-one — which was the first notable thing. The distribution was not random. He ran the dates against the reservation records Rafi maintained in the back office and found, after forty minutes of cross-referencing, that the eleven evenings with the anomalous signature were the eleven evenings on which a specific seating configuration had occurred: the cluster of tables seven through ten occupied simultaneously, the private dining room in use, and the bandstand at full seven-piece.

Maximum room. Maximum coverage. Maximum data.

The signature appeared on the evenings when the room was most interesting. He sat with this for a long time.

Interesting was not a technical term. It was, however, often the first sign that a technical explanation was waiting nearby.

Then he ran the frequency through his classification library — the full library, not just the baseline ambient file but the deeper archive, the classified archive, the one that contained the frequency signatures of every listening technology he had been briefed on and several he had not been briefed on but had reverse-engineered from field intercepts over eight years in the work.

No match.

He ran it against the open-source signals intelligence literature. No match.

He ran it against his own memory, which was the last resort and the most reliable instrument he possessed, because Jerome Park had heard a very large number of things in a very large number of rooms and almost nothing was entirely new.

Something stirred.

Not a match. Not a recognition. Something older than either of those — the specific unease of a system engineer looking at a design he had not built and could not fully read and understanding that it had been designed specifically to produce that feeling.

The sensation irritated him. Jerome disliked mysteries that appeared intentional.

This was not an amateur's frequency.

This was the output of something designed to be unclassifiable.

He thought about it for three days.

He thought about it the way he thought about difficult systems problems — continuously, in the background, while his hands and his face and the visible portion of his attention went on doing everything else. While he played the kit on Thursday evening with the same focus and the same musicianship and the same operational awareness the band always relied on.

While he assembled and disassembled the array in the post-service diagnostic. While he cooked breakfast on Saturday morning in his apartment four blocks from the restaurant and stared at the wall above the stove.

The problem followed him everywhere. Difficult problems often did.

On the fourth day he understood the architecture.

Not the source. Not yet. But the design principle — the engineering logic that had produced an unclassifiable frequency.

The signal was not transmitting intelligence.

He had established that before the first morning. The frequency carried no modulated data. It was not a transmission. Which meant it was not a collection device of the kind Jerome had built, which collected and stored. It was something older and more specific.

It was a marker.

A frequency signature designed to be present in a specific acoustic environment so that an external receiver — something outside the building, something passing by, something with the right decoder — could detect the presence of the marker and know, from its presence alone, that what the marker was attached to was active and in position.

Not what was being collected. Not the content. Just: yes. Still here. Still running. Still listening.

A heartbeat.

The elegance of it annoyed him almost as much as the intrusion itself.

Eleven times in forty-one evenings, something outside this building had passed close enough to receive confirmation that the device inside this building was operational.

Jerome sat with this understanding for exactly one hour. Then he went to find Seymour.

The Conversation: Saturday, 7:14 AM

He did not use the phone.

This was the first decision. The phone was not a secure instrument — not his phone, not any phone, because the architecture of the anomalous signal had already told him that whoever had placed the heartbeat frequency in this room understood signals at a level that made standard encryption a courtesy rather than a protection. There were situations in which caution became paranoia. Jerome did not believe this was one of them.

He went instead to the building, on a Saturday morning when the building was closed, and found Seymour in the basement rehearsal space where Seymour spent his Saturday mornings in the specific and solitary practice of a man who understood that musicianship required daily maintenance the way a surgical instrument required daily sharpening.

Seymour was playing Monk. He finished the phrase.

He looked up.

Jerome set his laptop on the lid of the piano.

"How long?" Seymour said, which was not the first question Jerome had expected but was, he understood, the correct first question from a man who processed operational intelligence the way Seymour processed it — sequentially, in order of consequence.

Not what. Not how. How long. Seymour always began with scope.

"Forty-one evenings," Jerome said. "Since opening night." Seymour looked at the screen.

He looked at it for a long time.

Jerome watched him and said nothing. He had learned, in the years of working with Seymour, that the silence was not absence but process — that what looked like stillness was in fact the fastest and most efficient thinking Jerome had ever observed in another person.

Seymour Emerson moved slowly because he had already arrived.

"It's a beacon," Seymour said. "Not a collector." "Yes."

"So we have a second collector somewhere in the room. Something we haven't found. The beacon is the proof of life for the collector."

"That's my read," Jerome said.

Hearing Seymour arrive at the same conclusion in under a minute was reassuring for reasons Jerome did not entirely examine.

"That's my read," Jerome said. "The beacon tells the external receiver that whatever is collecting is still operational. It's a status check."

"Passive."

"Entirely. No outbound transmission of content. Just presence confirmation." Seymour took his hands off the keys.

"Who else knows?"

"No one."

"Dianne needs to know today," Seymour said.

"Before this building opens for anything."

The Conversation: Saturday, 10:33 AM

Dianne listened without interrupting.

This was one of the qualities Jerome respected most about her — the ability to receive a complex technical briefing without the interpretive interference that most people injected into the listening process, the tendency to begin constructing responses before the information was complete. She listened the way she presumably listened in a clinical assessment: with the full weight of her attention and none of her conclusions.

It made people more precise around her. There was nowhere to hide a weak assumption or an unsupported leap. If the logic held, she would follow it. If it did not, she would find the break.

When Jerome finished, she was quiet for a moment. "Eleven evenings," she said. "Not every Thursday." "Correct."

"Which evenings?" Jerome had the list. He passed it across the table.

Dianne looked at it. She ran her finger down the dates. Her expression did not change but her stillness changed quality — the stillness shifted from receptive to analytical, the slight recalibration of a mind that had just received information that confirmed something it had already begun to suspect.

Jerome noticed Seymour notice it. Neither of them commented.

"These are the evenings the private dining room was in use," she said. Not a question.

"And tables seven through ten all occupied," Jerome said. "And full seven-piece on the bandstand."

She looked at Seymour.

"The evenings with the highest operational footprint."

"Yes," Seymour said.

"So whoever placed the beacon — and whoever is receiving its signal — knows the difference between a quiet Tuesday and a Thursday when we are fully operational." She set down the list.

"They are not monitoring the restaurant. They are monitoring the operation."

The basement room held that sentence for a moment. It altered the shape of the problem. A restaurant could be observed incidentally. An operation was observed intentionally.

"Jerome," she said. "The external receiver. What's its range?" Jerome had spent two days on this question. "The frequency characteristics tell me it needs line-of-sight proximity — probably within forty meters. More than that and the signal degrades below detection threshold."

"So the receiver passes by," Seymour said. "Or parks nearby. Or occupies one of the buildings directly adjacent." Jerome paused. "It doesn't need to be there for long. The beacon transmits the confirmation in a burst — sub-second, like what I found in the acoustic log. The receiver only needs to be in range long enough to catch the burst."

Dianne thought about this.

"How often does the burst transmit?" "Based on the eleven instances across forty-one evenings," Jerome said, "I'd estimate the beacon is triggered by a specific acoustic threshold. It fires when the room reaches a certain volume and frequency density — when the band is playing and the room is full and the conversation level is at its peak. The ambient noise provides cover. The burst is invisible in the acoustic environment because the acoustic environment is already dense."

The engineering impressed him even as he disliked it. Whoever had designed the system understood concealment at a professional level.

Seymour turned to face the piano and played a single chord — not a musical gesture but the physical equivalent of a thought completing itself.

“It’s hidden in the music,” he said.

“In the noise the music makes,” Jerome said. “Yes.”

Nobody in the room particularly enjoyed that conclusion. The music was the heart of the place. The idea that someone had chosen it as camouflage felt invasive in a way that was difficult to articulate.

What They Knew They knew this: A beacon device, origin unknown, had been transmitting status confirmations from somewhere inside the building on eleven evenings since opening. The transmissions were not carrying content — they were proof-of-life signals for a separate collection device, which Jerome had not yet located.

They knew the external receiver was mobile or proximate — within forty meters on the evenings it collected. They knew it was active on the busiest evenings, which meant whoever operated it knew the building’s schedule well enough to predict the high-operational Thursdays from the quieter nights.

They knew the beacon had been designed specifically to be unclassifiable by the technology Jerome was running.

Which meant whoever designed it knew what Jerome was running. Which was the piece that kept Jerome awake.

Not the existence of the beacon. Not even the existence of the collector. Those were technical problems. Technical problems could be solved.

Knowledge was different. Knowledge implied access.

Because the specifications of his array were not public. They were not filed anywhere. They existed in two places: in Jerome's mind, and in the technical documentation that had been shared with exactly four people for operational review.

The same four people who had access to Jerome's kit specifications were the same four people who appeared in the distribution list the President would later share with Dianne.

Jerome did not know this yet. But he suspected it.

He had designed a system that no one outside its operational chain should have been able to build around.

Someone had built around it.

Which meant someone had either seen the design or understood the designer. Jerome was not sure which possibility he disliked more.

What They Did Not Know They did not know where inside the building the beacon was located.

Jerome had spent six days running a systematic sweep with a handheld spectral analyzer, working from the bandstand outward, methodically, in the way he approached every problem: from the center of the known system toward its edges. He had swept the bandstand. The kitchen pass. The wine cellar. The private dining room.

Nothing.

The beacon's frequency was designed to be undetectable by a standard sweep — which he had expected, which was why he had spent two of the six days modifying his analyzer to detect in the specific band he had isolated from the acoustic archive.

Even then: nothing in the areas he had swept.

Which told him the beacon was not in the areas he had swept.

Jerome trusted negative results more than most people. A failed search still narrowed the world. Every place it wasn't made the remaining possibilities more valuable.

He had not yet swept the dining room floor itself.

He had not swept it because the dining room floor during a service week was never empty, never accessible for a full systematic sweep, never without guests or staff or the movement of chairs and tables and feet that would compromise the reading.

He needed the building empty.

He needed a night when the dining room held nothing but tables and candlesticks and the acoustic residue of three hundred evenings of music and conversation.

An old room never truly emptied. It simply became quiet enough to reveal itself.

He told Dianne this.

She said: "Tuesday. Four in the morning." He said: "I'll need three hours."

She said: "I'll be here."

Tuesday, 4:11 AM

The dining room at four in the morning was a different room.

Jerome had been in it at odd hours before — early mornings, the occasional post-service hour — but never at this specific depth of night, when the candles were long extinguished and the tables were bare and the room existed without its contents, without the guests and the music and the low warm light, in the spare and architectural honesty of a space that knew what it was without ornament.

The heart pine floors. The fourteen-foot ceilings. The plasterwork at the cornices. The round tables, chairs upturned. The bandstand empty, the piano covered, the kit disassembled and locked as Jerome always left it.

Without people, the room felt larger. Not emptier. Larger. As though the absence of voices allowed the architecture to speak in its own register.

Dianne sat at table four with a cup of coffee and watched him work.

She did not speak. She had brought a legal pad and was writing on it in the unhurried way of a woman for whom the middle of the night was not an unusual time to work, which for her it was not.

Jerome never asked what she wrote in those notebooks. The contents belonged to Dianne in the same way his signal archives belonged to him.

Jerome moved in a grid.

He had laid out the dining room floor in a twelve-by-twelve grid in his head, each square roughly two meters by two meters, and he moved through them systematically with the modified analyzer held at floor level, reading the spectral output on the display in his left hand. His right hand moved the sensor. His eyes were on the display. His face was the face of a man for whom this kind of work was not labor but pleasure — the focused, total-commitment expression of someone doing the thing they were specifically built to do.

To an outside observer it might have looked obsessive. To Jerome it felt restful.

At 4:47, in grid square G7 — which corresponded to the area beneath table seven — the display spiked.

Jerome stopped.

The room seemed to stop with him.

He crouched.

He ran the sensor across the underside of the table. Nothing.

He ran it across the chair closest to the wall. Nothing.

He ran it across the baseboard. The display spiked again.

There it was. Not the answer, but the edge of it.

He examined the baseboard with the penlight he carried in his inside pocket. It looked like every other section of baseboard in the dining room — original Federal-period millwork, painted the same cream as the walls, the paint layers of a century and a half visible at the edges where the wood had compressed and cracked with the seasonal expansion and contraction of an old building's breathing.

He looked at the paint layers.

He looked at the section of baseboard directly behind where Viktor Selin sat every Thursday.

The paint layers at one specific section — a twelve-centimeter span at seat height — were wrong.

Not wrong in color. Not wrong in texture. Wrong in depth.

The paint sat differently there — uniformly, without the slight irregularity of genuine age, the kind of uniformity that only appears when a surface has been painted recently and carefully over something that wasn't there before.

It was the sort of detail most people would never notice. Jerome had built an entire career on noticing such details.

Jerome took out his multitool.

He removed a section of baseboard three centimeters long.

Behind it: a device the size and approximate shape of a large vitamin capsule.

Dark metal, matte finish, no visible seams. A single wire, hair-thin, that ran through a gap in the original plaster and disappeared into the wall.

For a moment neither of them spoke.

Finding the device was not a surprise. Finding it exactly where the data suggested it should be brought a different kind of satisfaction.

He did not touch it.

He photographed it with the camera in the analyzer — six shots, three angles — and replaced the baseboard with the care of a man reseating something that needed to stay exactly where it was.

He stood.

He looked at Dianne.

She had put down her pen.

"Table seven," she said. It was not a question.

"The baseboard behind the chair," he said. "A transceiver — not just a beacon. It stores and transmits both. Whatever is said at table seven on Thursday evenings has been collected since before we opened."

Dianne was very still.

Jerome watched her process it — the clinical, unhurried, total-assessment stillness of a woman arriving at a conclusion she had been approaching from a distance and had now reached.

"Before we opened," she said.

"The device was placed during renovation," he said. "The paint match is close but not perfect. Someone with access to the building during construction."

Which meant planning. Money. Time. The sort of preparation that begins long before an operation officially exists.

Dianne looked at table seven.

At the chair Selin always occupied. At the baseboard behind it.

“And the external receiver,” she said. “The thing that collects the transmission.”

“Mobile,” Jerome said. “Passes within forty meters on the high-footprint evenings. Based on the burst timing I recovered from the archive—” He checked his notes.

“—the collection has been consistent within a fourteen-minute window. Eight forty-seven to nine-oh-one PM.” “The first song,” Dianne said. “We’re always in the first song at eight forty-seven.”

“Which means the room is full. The band is loud. The cover is maximum.” She looked at him.

“Can you clone it?” There it was: the question that moved them from discovery to strategy.

Jerome had anticipated this question. It was the right question — the only question, the question that converted a liability into an asset.

“I can clone the beacon signal,” he said. “Replicate the heartbeat frequency exactly. The external receiver will continue to confirm the device as active.”

“While you disable the storage.”

“While I disable the storage,” he said. “The device goes deaf. The receiver continues to hear its heartbeat. From the outside, nothing has changed.”

The elegance of the solution appealed to him. Not because it was clever, but because it turned the device's greatest strength into a vulnerability.

Dianne stood.

She picked up her legal pad.

She looked at the room — at all of it, from the bandstand to the private dining room door, from the wine cellar stairs to the front entrance, from table four to table seven and the baseboard behind the chair that had been listening since before she had sat at the first table and decided this room was what she had been building toward.

"How long to implement?" she said. "One hour," Jerome said.

"When?" "Tonight if you want."

She looked at table seven one more time.

Her eyes lingered there briefly. Not on the table itself, but on the idea of it — the knowledge that something foreign had occupied a place she considered part of her room.

"Not tonight," she said. "We need to know who is receiving first. We need to identify the mobile unit." She turned to face him.

"Can you detect the receiver's presence in real time? When it's in range?" Jerome had also anticipated this question.

"I can build a directional detector," he said. "Something that will tell me when the external receiver is within range and give me a bearing. I can have it running inside the kit by Thursday."

Dianne nodded. "Thursday," she said. "Thursday," he said.

She looked at her watch. It was five twenty-three in the morning. "Jerome," she said.

"Yes."

"Good work."

He accepted this in the way he accepted all direct acknowledgment — briefly, without display, with the specific economy of a man who did not need praise to know when he had done something right.

Nevertheless, he appreciated it. Coming from Dianne, praise was never casual currency.

"The device has been listening since opening night," he said. "Every Thursday. Every conversation at that table. Every song."

He paused.

"Everything we gave that room — it heard." Dianne looked at the room one last time.

"Good," she said. "Then we know what it knows."

It was a practical answer. It was also, Jerome suspected, the only answer available to someone who loved the room as much as she did.

She turned and walked toward the kitchen, her legal pad in her hand, already writing.

Jerome stood alone in the dining room for a moment. He looked at the baseboard behind table seven. He looked at his kit, covered and locked at the bandstand.

He thought about forty-one evenings of music filling this room, of Seymour's piano and Freeman's guitar and Dianne's voice and the specific sound of a room being what it was built to be — beautiful, warm, safe, entirely itself.

And beneath all of it, since the first evening, this: a device in a baseboard listening to everything.

The violation irritated him more than he expected. Not because it threatened the operation. Because it had occupied something he respected.

He thought about what it had heard.

He thought about what it was going to hear next. He thought: we know what it knows.

He thought: it does not know what we know.

For the first time since discovering the beacon, he allowed himself a brief moment of satisfaction. The advantage had changed hands.

He covered the analyzer and picked up his kit bag and left.

The building stood at the corner of M and Wisconsin in the dark before dawn, holding its secrets the way it had held everything since 1887.

It knew how.

Chapter Two: Thursday

The reservation said eight o'clock. He arrived at seven fifty-three.

Dianne noted it from the second floor landing before she descended — the particular punctuality of a man who wanted to appear casual about time and had overcorrected by seven minutes. She filed it beside everything else she had filed about Viktor Selin: the way he held a menu he'd already decided about, the European placement of his napkin, the forty-three minutes of watching that he had dressed as appreciation.

She had accumulated dozens of these observations by now. Individually they meant very little. Together they formed the outline of a man who was becoming increasingly difficult to dismiss as merely another regular customer.

She did not go down immediately. She watched him be seated — the corner table, as the card had promised — and watched him take the room in the way he always took rooms: the slow, appreciative scan that was neither slow nor appreciative.

He was cataloguing. Exits, sightlines, faces. He did it in four seconds and then picked up his water glass and became, again, simply a man having dinner.

Four seconds was good. She had trained people who couldn't do it in ten. She had also trained people who could do it in two. Viktor lived somewhere between competence and expertise, which made him interesting.

She descended at eight o'clock precisely.

Rafi was already at his table.

He was always already at his table — table four, near the interior wall, positioned at the exact center of the room's financial geography, which was how he thought about rooms: in terms of the money moving through them and what that money said about the people carrying it. He had been this way since he was nine years old, growing up three houses down from Dianne in a neighborhood in New Orleans where understanding the economics of a room was not an intellectual exercise but a survival skill.

Three houses down had been the architecture of his entire life. It was the distance at which he had learned to love — far enough to respect the separateness of another person's world, close enough to know every sound that crossed between the houses, every radio station, every argument and celebration and the particular quality of a Tuesday afternoon when nothing was happening and the street smelled like cut grass and river water and everything was ordinary in the way that, he understood now, only an ordinary childhood can be.

Memory softened many things. It had never softened those afternoons. They remained exactly as they were, preserved with an almost unreasonable clarity.

He had not had an ordinary adulthood. Neither had she.

He had a glass of Meursault and a leather notebook that appeared to contain wine notes. It did not contain wine notes.

On the right-hand pages tonight: the ownership structures of fourteen shell companies he had traced through four jurisdictions in the past seventy-two hours, all of which connected, through pathways of considerable ingenuity, to a single account in a private bank in Liechtenstein that had been opened eleven months ago — one month before Viktor Selin's posting to Washington had been announced through official channels.

Whoever had built the structure was intelligent. That was obvious. The question was whether the intelligence belonged to the owner of the money or to someone hired to hide it.

On the left-hand pages, in the smaller, more private handwriting that he used when he was writing the other thing: a record of what Dianne had said during the soundcheck that afternoon — two words, spoken to nobody in particular, standing at the microphone while Seymour played the opening bars of Autumn Leaves.

She had said there it is in the voice of someone recognizing something. She had not said what it was. She had not looked as though she expected anyone to have heard her. Rafi had heard her.

He had written it down, as he wrote everything down, with the date and the time and a notation in his own private shorthand that meant: another degree of return. Still approaching. Hold.

Eleven years had taught him patience. Not perfect patience. But enough.

The Liechtenstein account was frightened. It was over-engineered in the way that only truly frightened money is over-engineered — too many layers, too many cutouts, the financial equivalent of a man who checks the lock three times before he sleeps.

He sipped his Meursault and traced his finger down the column of shell companies and thought about fear — the financial kind and the other kind, the kind that lived in the space between she does not remember me and the Tuesday that was coming, that was always coming, that had been coming for eleven years, when she would.

Or would not. That possibility still existed. He simply refused to live as though it were the most likely outcome.

Seymour arrived at the bandstand at eight-fifteen with the unhurried authority of a man who had never been late to anything in his life and considered the concept of rushing a form of intellectual failure.

In Seymour's experience, most mistakes entered a room at speed. He had built an entire life around arriving at the correct place before urgency became necessary.

He sat at the piano, adjusted the bench, and ran a single quiet chord that the dining room heard as a musician warming up and his band heard as: we are live, we are recording, all systems are active.

Tonight the bandstand held seven.

Marcus Webb on bass — though on the nights Dixie played, Marcus moved to the edge of the stage and watched the room with the particular attention of a behavioral linguist reading a crowd. Tonight was Dixie's night and Marcus was where he was supposed to be.

Dixie St. James stood at the upright bass with the settled authority of a woman who knew exactly what the instrument required and had made peace with that requirement a long time ago. She wore deep green. Her ring — because she wore the ring, as they all wore the ring — was warm against her left hand on the neck of the bass.

Celeste Okafor on trumpet, standing at the edge of the bandstand with the stillness of a woman conserving something.

Celeste's stillness often misled people. They mistook it for passivity when it was actually preparation.

Jerome Park at the drums, the kit alive with what the room could not see and the band knew was there.

The new detector was running. Hidden, silent, waiting. Jerome gave no indication of it, but part of his attention remained attached to the system at all times.

Freeman Freeman on a low stool to Seymour's left, his guitar across his lap and his harmonica in his shirt pocket — present, unhurried, watching the room with the trained attention of a man who had written his dissertation on exactly this: how groups hold together when the pressure arrives.

Stephon Keyes at the Hammond B3, which sat to the right of Seymour's piano like a larger, more emphatic version of the same idea. His hands rested on the keys in the posture of a man who was not playing yet but was already inside the music, already in the conversation, already three bars ahead of wherever the song was going.

Stephon always looked relaxed before a set. The people who knew him best understood that relaxation was simply the visible surface of intense concentration.

Seymour looked at his band. His band looked back.

He played the opening bars of Autumn Leaves and the dining room exhaled and became what it always became when Seymour began.

The transition happened every night and still felt faintly miraculous. A restaurant became a room. A room became a gathering. A gathering became something closer to a community.

Miss Dianne sang three times on a Thursday.

This was not policy. It was not listed anywhere or announced. It was simply what happened, the way certain things happen in certain rooms — organically, inevitably, as though the room itself required it.

Regulars knew the rhythm without consciously knowing it. First song. Then later, something brighter. Then the final song near closing, the one people carried home with them.

The first song came at nine o'clock precisely.

Seymour felt her before he saw her — the shift in the room's atmosphere that Dianne's approach to the stage always created, a change in barometric pressure that was not metaphor but fact. He modulated without looking up, his left hand moving into the opening figure. Stephon felt it too — his hands lifted from the Hammond keys and found the piano's upper register instead, the B3 stepping back to make room for what was coming, the way a large man steps back to let something important through.

They had performed together long enough that these adjustments no longer required discussion. The music moved first. The musicians followed.

Dianne stepped onto the stage in ivory silk and stood at the microphone with the stillness of a woman who had nothing to prove and everything to give.

The room went quiet.

Behind her, without announcement or fanfare, the three took their places.

Freeman shifted on his stool, his guitar across his lap, his eyes on Dianne's back. Dixie adjusted her stance at the bass, her bow hand dropping to her side, her voice ready. Tamara appeared at the edge of the stage in midnight blue — not on it, not quite, standing at the border between the floor and the performance in the way she occupied all borders, belonging to both sides simultaneously.

For a brief moment the four women formed a composition that looked almost staged, though nothing about it was. The room noticed before it understood why it was noticing.

Dianne looked out at her room.

She found Selin without appearing to find him. She sang.

I'd Rather Go Blind.

Seymour's piano beneath her was the question the song asked. Stephon's left hand found a low note on the Hammond and held it — not playing, sustaining, a single tone that lived beneath everything else like the ground itself. Jerome played brushes on the snare with the lightness of a man who understood that some songs require the drums to almost disappear.

The room settled deeper into itself. Conversations ended not because anyone requested silence but because the song made other activities seem less important.

Freeman came in on the second verse.

He didn't announce it. His voice arrived beneath Dianne's the way a hand arrives beneath something falling — quietly, completely, with total commitment to the catch. The harmony he chose was not the obvious one. It was the one that lived a third below her note and made her voice suddenly larger, suddenly more inevitable, suddenly the thing the room had been moving toward all evening without knowing it.

Seymour heard several people look up. Not physically at first, but internally — the subtle shift that happens when a listener realizes a song has become something larger than it was a moment ago.

Dixie came in a beat behind Freeman. Her alto sat under his baritone the way her bass sat under the band's harmonic structure — holding the architecture from underneath, invisible until you tried to imagine the sound without it.

Dixie understood support as both a musical and personal discipline. She rarely reached for attention. The result was that attention often found her anyway.

And Tamara, at the edge of the stage, added the voice that completed it — not loud, not forward, but present in the way that a load-bearing wall is present: you don't see it doing its work but you feel the room stand up straighter because it's there.

The four voices together — Dianne's lead, Freeman's third, Dixie's deep foundation, Tamara's fill — were something the room had not heard before and would not forget.

Even the band felt it. Not surprise exactly. Recognition. The arrangement had always seemed possible. Tonight it finally seemed real.

Viktor Selin, at table seven, had stopped pretending to look at anything other than the stage.

His face had opened in the way that faces open when they are ambushed by something genuine. His training had no category for this. His training was good and it had no category for this.

He remained aware of the room. Years of habit made that unavoidable. But awareness had moved into the background. The music occupied the foreground now.

Dianne sang the last verse with everything she had. The room came back to itself slowly.

The applause began in the chest before it reached the hands.

It arrived in waves rather than all at once, as though people needed a moment to remember where they were before responding.

The second song came at ten o'clock and it was a different proposition entirely.

Seymour announced it the way he announced certain songs — not with words but with a groove, a rolling boogie figure in the left hand that began so naturally it seemed to have been there all along.

Stephon found it immediately on the Hammond, the Leslie speaker engaging with a warmth that changed the room's temperature by some social degree. Jerome cracked the snare on two and four. Freeman pulled his harmonica from his shirt pocket, ran a quick blues scale that was also a hello and also a warning, and then put it back.

A few regulars smiled the moment they heard it. They knew that sound. They knew what usually followed.

He picked up his guitar instead.

He played four bars alone — just the guitar, just Freeman, a rhythm figure so deep in the pocket it seemed to come from below the floor — and then Seymour's left hand locked in and the band found the groove the way the band always found the groove: all at once, completely, as though they had been there all along and were simply making it visible.

The transition was so clean it felt less like musicians entering a song than a photograph coming into focus.

Dianne came to the microphone with a different face. Not the excavator. The instigator.

Got my mojo working.

And then the room got its theater.

Tamara had been mid-conversation with a Norwegian trade attaché when the groove started. She paused in the middle of a sentence, held up one finger in the universal language of forgive me, this cannot wait, and stood.

The attaché laughed before she even reached the stage. He had learned enough about Thursday nights to recognize inevitability when he saw it.

She moved the way she moved when she was not performing movement but had become it — the NYU training alive in every line of her body, the stage instinct that never fully went dormant igniting all at once.

From the service corridor, James the waiter appeared at the edge of the stage. Twenty-seven, impossibly graceful, the Howard theater degree he'd mentioned to nobody during his interview alive in every movement.

James always claimed he was "just helping out."

Nobody who had seen him move believed that for a second.

He and Tamara found each other across the room by instinct and rhythm and the particular recognition of two people who speak the same language and are glad to find each other.

But tonight there was something more. Freeman Freeman stepped off his stool.

He took the harmonica out of his pocket and played eight bars walking toward the front of the stage — the harmonica a human voice unto itself, laughing and pleading and crowing all at once — and then he planted himself at the edge of the stage and let it rip. His whole body was in it.

His feet on the floor, his shoulders, the way his head went back on the high notes. He had been in churches in Shreveport where the music did this to a room and he had been on stages in New York and Chicago and London where it did this to a room and he had never fully distinguished between those contexts because he didn't think the distinction was real.

Music that was true was music that was true.

Dixie was still at her bass but her voice had come forward — her alto rising behind Dianne in the chorus with the muscular warmth of a woman who knew exactly how to fill the register beneath a lead vocal and make the whole thing sound twice as large as it was. She was moving, too — not dancing, not exactly, but her body was in the music the way her body was always in the music: the groove lived in her hips, the beat in her shoulders, the joy of it visible in the way that joy is only visible in people who feel it rather than perform it.

Marcus, watching from the edge of the stage, smiled despite himself. Dixie always looked most like herself when she forgot anyone might be watching.

Tamara and James were extraordinary together. The room abandoned its dinner.

Even the former Secretary of State was laughing — genuinely, fully, the laugh of a man caught off guard by joy.

Several tables had stopped pretending to eat altogether. Glasses remained lifted halfway to mouths. Forks rested untouched beside plates. The room had collectively decided that dinner could wait.

At table seven, Viktor Selin was smiling.

The second real smile of the evening.

Not the diplomatic smile. Not the social smile. The involuntary one. The smile that arrives before its owner has had the opportunity to approve it.

Dianne sang the last verse directly to the room — to all of it — with the total generosity of a woman who understood that the gift of a song was not diminished by the work it was also doing.

The groove resolved.

The room erupted.

For a few seconds the applause was less applause than release — the room returning energy it had been holding onto for the duration of the song.

Freeman took a bow that was really a prayer. Tamara curtsied. Dixie shook her head slowly at her strings, the private gesture of a musician who has just done something she's pleased with.

Jerome laughed quietly from behind the kit. He had seen that gesture before. It usually meant Dixie would spend the next hour claiming the performance had been merely acceptable.

The Norwegian attaché decided he would be at Miss Dianne's every Thursday for the foreseeable future.

He would later tell three different people that the decision had been made during the second chorus. By midnight he would be convinced it had happened much earlier.

The third song came at eleven, and it came the way the last song of an evening always comes — as a gift and a benediction, the thing the room had been moving toward without knowing it.

The room knew the evening was drawing to a close. You could feel it in the attention. The energy was still present, but it had softened around the edges.

Seymour played the opening figure of Harvest Moon alone first.

Just the piano. Just that melody — simple, open, the particular musical honesty of a song that has no interest in impressing anyone, that only wants to stand in the night air and look up.

Seymour loved songs that refused to show off. Age had only deepened that preference.

Then Stephon came in on the Hammond.

Not the full register — the tender part of it, the upper manual played soft, the Leslie turning slowly, the sound of it like something breathing. He found the space beneath Seymour's melody and filled it the way good light fills a room: without calling attention to itself, without taking anything, only adding warmth to what was already there.

Freeman reached for his guitar and played the chord that completed the picture — a quiet, open voicing, the strings barely touched, the sound more suggestion than statement.

Jerome brushed the ride cymbal in a pattern so gentle it was almost silence organized.

The room received it the way rooms receive certain things when they have been properly prepared — with the full weight of their attention, with the willingness to be moved.

The transition from the exuberance of the previous number to this quiet openness should have felt abrupt. Somehow it never did.

Dianne's voice on Harvest Moon was different from both songs that had preceded it. Not the excavator and not the instigator. Something quieter.

Something that lived closer to the bone. The voice of a woman who had stopped performing for the night and was simply, for these few minutes, present — in her room, in her body, in the unexplained sense of homecoming that this building gave her every time she stood on this stage.

There were evenings when she felt the sensation more strongly than others. Tonight it sat around her like familiar weather.

Come a little bit closer, hear what I have to say.

Tamara came in first behind her.

She found the harmony she always found on this song — not the closest third, not the comfortable choice, but the one that lived in the space between intimacy and ache, the harmony that said I am here, I have always been here without using any of those words. On this song more than any other, Tamara's voice behind Dianne's was the sound of the thing the novel was actually about — the friendship that crossed the amnesia, the love that did not require the beloved to remember it in order to be true.

Somewhere in the room, people heard friendship. Others heard loyalty. A few heard grief. The arrangement allowed each listener to find their own way into it.

Freeman came in on the second verse — his baritone dropping beneath Tamara's harmony and beneath Dianne's lead, a third voice that made the arrangement suddenly complete, that gave it the depth of a chord rather than the linearity of a melody.

The addition was subtle enough that several listeners could not have identified the exact moment it happened. They only knew the song had somehow become larger.

Dixie came in last.

Her alto was barely above a whisper on this song. She had made this decision herself, without discussion — had understood from the first time she heard Dianne sing Harvest Moon that this song required something under the surface rather than above it, a low foundation hum that you felt more than heard, the musical equivalent of the ground itself being present.

Dixie had always trusted understatement. Some musicians filled every available space. She preferred to strengthen the structure from underneath and let the song decide how much of her to reveal.

The four voices together on Harvest Moon were the sound of something irreplaceable.

The candles had burned to their final hour. The room had thinned to its most devoted remainder. The guests who understood that the last hour of a great evening was its most valuable, that the point of dinner was never really the food, had stayed. Everyone else had gone home full and warm and already making plans to return.

The room felt different during this last hour. Less like a restaurant and more like a gathering of people who had accidentally discovered they had been sharing the same experience all evening.

Viktor Selin was still at table seven.

He had been there for three hours and eleven minutes and had not once looked at his watch.

Dianne noticed. She noted his stillness — the particular stillness of a man who had forgotten he was supposed to be somewhere else, who had been brought, by music and warmth and the specific genius of this room, to the threshold of threshold. The place where the performance of not-feeling gives way.

She had seen versions of this before. Not often, but enough to recognize it. The moment when a person stopped managing their experience and simply had it.

She held the last note.

Freeman held his harmony beneath it. Tamara held hers.

Dixie held the floor.

Seymour let the piano resolve.

Stephon let the Hammond breathe out slowly, the Leslie decelerating, the sound diminishing like something walking away through a field at dusk.

Freeman's guitar rang the last chord and let it die naturally — no cutoff, no gesture, just the sound finding its own end in the room's warm air. The song was over.

The room sat in it for a moment. Then, gently, it returned.

Nobody wanted to be the first person to break the spell. The applause, when it came, arrived carefully, almost apologetically, as though the room understood that something delicate had just passed through it.

Rafi, at table four, sat with his hands still and his notebook closed and his Meursault untouched and let himself be, briefly and completely, in the only place he was.

He looked at the stage.

She was still at the microphone — not singing, simply standing in the last of the song's light, in the room's warmth, with the particular stillness of a woman who had given something real and was letting the giving settle before she moved again. Her hands were at her sides. Her ring caught the candlelight.

There were evenings when she seemed tired afterward, and evenings when she seemed energized. Tonight she looked neither. Tonight she looked present.

He had been watching her stand in rooms for eleven years without her knowing what the watching meant to him.

Longer, if you counted the neighborhood — and he counted the neighborhood, because the neighborhood was where it had begun, in the way that most things that lasted began: quietly, without announcement, in the ordinary proximity of two people whose houses happened to be three doors apart on a street in New Orleans that smelled like night-blooming jasmine in the summer and red beans on Mondays and the river always, underneath everything, the river.

Memory had polished some details and sharpened others. The river remained exactly as he remembered it. So did the distance between the houses.

He had loved her since before he had the vocabulary for it. This was the fact he had been the most honest about in the seventeen notebooks — more honest about it there than he had been with anyone living, including Tamara, who knew most of it and understood the rest.

The notebooks had become a kind of parallel life. Not an alternative to reality, but a record of the reality he could not discuss anywhere else.

What he had written, in the seventh notebook, on a Thursday not unlike this one: The clinical word for what I am doing is witnessing.

I am witnessing her return to herself the way you witness a patient emerging from a long unconsciousness — slowly, in stages, the self assembling from the available materials. The difference is that I knew the self before it went under.

I know what it is returning to. I am, in this specific and unreplicable way, the only person in the world who can confirm the arrival when it comes.

I am waiting to confirm the arrival.

I have been waiting for eleven years. I would wait eleven more.

Even now, rereading the entry months later, he had not found a single sentence he wanted to change.

He thought about the photograph twelve steps below — two girls on a porch, one pointing, one laughing, the summer they were sixteen and they had taken it with Tamara's mother's Polaroid and Dianne had written their names on the white border in her careful, slanted handwriting, and the handwriting had faded, which was fine, because the photograph had not faded, and he still had his copy in a frame on his desk that he had never moved, not once, in twenty-five years.

Some objects became important because of what they represented. Others became important because they had survived. The photograph managed to do both.

He thought about the lot behind the building — cleared, fenced, patient — and about the footnote on the last page of Volume Fifteen.

He thought: not yet.

He thought: but the room is almost ready.

He thought: she is almost ready.

The distinction mattered. The room and Dianne were moving toward the same destination, but not necessarily at the same speed.

Then he picked up his glass.

He drank.

He opened his notebook to the left-hand page and wrote, in the small private handwriting: There it is. She said it again tonight. Still approaching. Closer.

He dated it.

He closed it.

The evening was not over yet.

End of Chapter Two

Below the dining room, in the war room twelve steps down, the photograph sat in the center of the round table in the dark.

Two girls on a porch in New Orleans. One pointing.

One laughing.

The photograph seemed almost luminous in the low amber light. Not because it reflected more light than anything else in the room, but because so much attention had been paid to it over the years. Memory has a way of making certain objects feel brighter than they are.

The Hammond's last note had found its way through the floor and into the room below and had hung in the air above the photograph for a moment before the building absorbed it.

The amber light burned steady. The tunnel waited.

It always waited. Patiently. Without urgency. The tunnel had been built for movement, but most of its existence was spent in anticipation.

Outside on the corner of M and Wisconsin, October moved through the city the way October always moved through Washington — with the particular authority of a season that knows its time is short and means to be felt.

The building stood at the corner and held its light. It had been holding light since 1887.

It knew how.

Buildings survived by learning the difference between what should be remembered and what should be endured. This one had become unusually skilled at both.

Chapter Three: What The Tunnel Knows

The wine cellar was cool and smelled of oak and time. The bottles in their cradles watched the ceiling.

The room had its own gravity. Conversations slowed down here. Decisions acquired weight. Even people encountering it for the first time tended to lower their voices without knowing why.

Dianne spoke first.

She always spoke first when she was running a briefing, and she was always running a briefing, and everybody in every room she had ever stood in understood this about her without being told. It was not a power move. It was simply the natural order of a mind that had already completed its analysis before anyone else had finished asking the question.

Years earlier, before the accident, people had occasionally mistaken this habit for impatience. The people who knew her well understood it was the opposite. Dianne listened carefully. She simply processed quickly.

"We have a second operation running in our room," she said. "On our target. Using equipment we don't have access to, which means they have a budget we don't know about or a technology pipeline we haven't been briefed on."

She looked at Rafi.

Rafi set his notebook on the wine cellar table. "The card confirm at table eleven tells me their asset reported active contact tonight," he said. "They are not watching Selin the way we are watching Selin. They are watching us watch Selin. We are their intelligence."

The silence that followed lasted exactly long enough to mean something. Tamara shifted her weight against the wine rack. Seymour folded his hands. Nobody challenged the conclusion because nobody could find a weakness in it.

"Seymour," Dianne said.

"The frequency is clean," Seymour said. "Too clean. Whoever designed it knew what kind of array to hide from. They knew the specs of our equipment."

He looked at Jerome.

Jerome had been standing at the end of the wine cellar table in the specific stillness he occupied when he was not playing — which was the same stillness he occupied when he was playing, because Jerome Park had one mode and it was total focus. He had a tablet in his hand. On the screen: the spectral readout from the directional detector he had built into the kit four days ago, which had confirmed tonight — during the second song, during the window between eight forty-seven and nine-oh-one — the presence of the external receiver.

The graph looked harmless. Most consequential information did. A lifetime of intelligence work had taught Jerome that danger rarely announced itself visually.

"The receiver was a vehicle," he said. "Street level. Moving east on M Street. It passed twice within the collection window. Second pass collected the burst."

"The baseboard device transmitted on schedule?" Dianne said.

"On schedule and clean. The clone is holding." Jerome set the tablet on the table. "From outside, nothing has changed. The device they planted reads as fully operational. The heartbeat is regular. Their receiver has no reason to suspect the storage is disabled."

Tamara, who had been leaning against a wine rack with her arms crossed, looked from Jerome to Dianne. "How long has it been deaf?" "Since Wednesday night," Dianne said. "Four days."

"Four Thursdays of collection they don't know they've lost," Tamara said.

There was satisfaction in the observation, but only a small amount. Too much remained unknown for celebration.

"Three weeks," Jerome said. "The disable went in three weeks before the Thursday of the Selin operation."

"Which means," Rafi said, "everything Selin said at that table tonight — every word of the false intelligence Dianne delivered — went nowhere."

"Nowhere except where we sent it," Dianne said. "Through Selin. Up the chain. In the direction it was designed to travel."

She looked at the door in the west wall. The door with two locks and a code that changed every seventy-two hours.

Her eyes lingered there briefly. The room beyond contained answers. Whether those answers would be useful remained to be seen.

"The device in the baseboard is no longer a liability," she said. "It is evidence. It tells us the renovation timeline, the construction access, the specific technical specifications that were shared with the person who designed around Jerome's array." She paused. "It has been there since before we opened. Whoever placed it knew what this building was going to be before we built it."

The wine cellar counted its bottles.

Nobody missed the significance of that statement. Planning measured in months was ordinary. Planning measured in years belonged to a different category of adversary entirely.

"So," Tamara said, with the particular precision she deployed when she wanted a room to understand she was not asking a question but opening a verdict. "Someone knew what this building was going to be before we built it."

"Yes," Dianne said.

"Are we saying what I think we're saying?" Tamara asked.

Her tone was calm. That was usually when she was most dangerous. Tamara rarely raised her voice when she was angry. She preferred accuracy.

"We're saying that Operation Meridian has been compromised," Dianne said.

"We don't know by whom. We don't know how deep. We know that someone planted a device in this building that was collecting the same intelligence we were collecting — and that Jerome found it, identified it, cloned it, and turned it into the most important piece of forensic evidence we have."

She looked at Jerome.

He received this without display.

Praise always seemed to land somewhere internal with Jerome. You never saw the reaction. You simply noticed that he heard it.

"What we know now," Dianne continued, "that we didn't know an hour ago: the receiver is vehicular. It moves. It operates on a schedule tied to our service calendar. And it collected forty-one evenings before Jerome found it."

"Forty-one evenings of everything said at table seven," Tamara said.

"Everything said at table seven," Jerome confirmed. "Every guest. Every conversation. Every song."

A different silence. Different weight.

Forty-one evenings was no longer a number. It was a measure of exposure. Every person in the room was doing the arithmetic privately.

"The President needs to know tonight," she said. "And we need to know what he knows."

She crossed to the door. Produced the first key from inside her jacket — ivory silk, no visible pocket, the key simply appeared in her hand the way things appeared in Dianne's hands when she needed them.

The second key she wore at her throat. What the room had taken all evening for a pendant of no particular significance was a key cut to a tolerance of three microns by a machinist who worked in a building that appeared on no public map.

She removed it. Turned it.

Tamara had seen the gesture dozens of times and still found it faintly theatrical. Dianne would have objected to the description. That did not make it less true.

The code she entered from memory. The door opened.

The Corridor: 9:41 PM The corridor ran west beneath Georgetown Drive Drive and it was nothing like the building above it.

Above was warmth and gold light and the smell of good food and better wine and the last of Seymour's music finding its way into every corner.

Below was climate-controlled certainty — white walls, LED lighting calibrated for visual acuity, floors of sealed concrete that carried footsteps without echo.

The kind of space designed not for comfort but for clarity. The transition always felt abrupt, even to people who used the corridor regularly. One world ended at the door. Another began immediately beyond it.

They walked in the order they always walked the tunnel. Dianne first.

Rafi at her left shoulder. Tamara behind.

Seymour at the rear with the loose-limbed, unhurried movement of a large man entirely comfortable in confined spaces — which had not always been true and had been addressed during eighteen months of training he preferred not to discuss.

Seymour had once described those eighteen months as "educational" and then declined every follow-up question. Nobody had pressed him.

The corridor was four hundred meters. They walked it in five minutes. Nobody spoke.

This was the corridor's effect on all of them — it produced silence the way cathedrals produce silence, not by demanding it but by being the kind of space that made talk feel beside the point. The four of them had walked this corridor together a dozen times and had never once filled it with unnecessary words.

The tunnel encouraged reflection. More accurately, it left no room to avoid it.

At the end, a single door. A single lock. A code that was not changed on any schedule Dianne had been given.

She knocked.

Three beats. Two. One.

The door opened from the other side.

The Room at the End of the Tunnel: 9:46 PM Cartwright opened the door.

He was the President's man — which in Washington was a specific species of absolute loyalty that expressed itself not through enthusiasm but through an almost geological stillness. He had no first name in any context Dianne had ever operated in. He was sixty, grey, and had eyes that processed information the way a lens processes light — completely, without distortion, and with total indifference to what it found.

Tamara had spent three years trying to determine whether Cartwright possessed a sense of humor. The evidence remained inconclusive.

He stood aside.

They entered.

The room was spare. A table. Six chairs. A screen on the far wall currently dark. A phone that had never been used for anything so mundane as a call. The air was drier here, more carefully filtered — the air of a space where important things were said and the atmosphere itself had been engineered not to judge them.

Nothing in the room was decorative. Everything had a purpose. Even the absence of decoration felt intentional.

The President was already seated.

He was smaller in person than on television.

This was the thing everyone noticed and nobody said, because it seemed impolite to observe that the most powerful person in the world occupied less physical space than the idea of him. But he carried the office the way certain people carry grief or certainty — not visibly, not as performance, but as a quality of presence that preceded him into every room and remained after he left.

Power often announced itself loudly. The President's version rarely needed to.

He did not stand when they entered. He did not need to.

“Sit down,” he said.

The voice was what television preserved accurately — low, unhurried, the voice of a man who had learned that speed was for people who weren't sure they would be listened to.

They sat.

Cartwright remained at the door.

The President looked at each of them in turn with the quality of attention that Dianne recognized and respected — the attention of someone who reads people not for pleasure but because the information is load-bearing. His eyes rested on Dianne last and longest. Not favoritism. Expectation. There was a difference, and both of them understood it.

"Tell me what you found," he said.

She told him.

She told it the way she told everything — completely, in order, without editorializing, the facts arranged in the structure that made their meaning clearest. The frequency. The card confirm at table eleven. The device that had been in the building since construction. The distribution list of seven.

Nobody interrupted. They had all heard Dianne brief before. Questions came afterward. During the briefing itself, interruption usually created less clarity rather than more.

She told it in four minutes and twelve seconds. She knew because she counted.

The room was quiet when she finished — the quiet of a space in which the information has changed the shape of everything and the people in it are deciding what the new shape requires.

Rafi watched the President carefully. Not for the obvious reactions. The useful information was almost always in the reactions people believed they had successfully concealed.

The President did not react immediately. Dianne read the micro expressions crossing his face the way she read everything — precisely, without commentary, each one filed against what she already knew. Some of what she saw was new to him.

Some of it was not.

That distinction interested her more than any single expression. Surprise had a shape. Confirmation had a different one.

He looked at the table.

He looked up.

"I know about the device," he said.

The room absorbed this.

Even Seymour blinked once. For Seymour, that was approximately equivalent to most people standing up.

Tamara's hands were still in her lap. Rafi's face had done nothing.

Seymour was looking at the middle distance in the way he looked at the middle distance when he was solving something that had more than one correct answer and needed to determine which correctness was required.

Dianne said: "How long?" "Six weeks," the President said. "We found the frequency six weeks ago. We didn't pull it because we needed to know who was listening."

The answer landed differently than an admission would have. It contained justification before anyone had asked for one.

"You used our operation to run a counter-operation," Dianne said.

It was not an accusation. It was the clinical observation of a fact, delivered without heat because heat was not the instrument the moment required.

“Yes,” the President said. “And table eleven?” “Cartwright’s people. Watching the watchers.” A silence of considerable density.

Tamara leaned back slightly. One question had been answered. Three new ones had arrived to replace it.

Dianne said: “So the question is not who planted the device. The question is who they’re reporting to. And whether that person is on the distribution list.”

“Yes,” the President said. “And you don’t know.”

“I have a candidate,” the President said. “I am not prepared to act on a candidate. Acting on a candidate at this level, without certainty, does more damage than the leak itself.”

Nobody in the room disagreed. At this altitude, mistakes propagated outward for years.

He leaned forward.

“I need certainty,” he said. “That is why you’re here. That is why you built the room upstairs. That is why Viktor Selin is sitting at table seven right now, three hours into an evening he came to for reasons he doesn’t fully understand.” He paused. “I don’t need you to turn Selin anymore. Selin is the mechanism, not the target. I need you to use him.”

The sentence settled over the room.

Rafi wrote nothing down. The phrasing was too important to risk paraphrasing.

“Use him as what?” Tamara asked.

The President looked at her with what might, in a different context, have been appreciation.

“Bait,” he said. “I need to feed information through Selin — specific, verifiable, false — and watch where it goes. When it surfaces, in whatever form it surfaces, it will carry the fingerprints of whoever on that list is passing our intelligence to the device in your dining room."

Dianne was quiet.

She was doing what she did when the problem required everything she had — the forensic psychology, the neuropsychological profiling, the thirty years of reading human beings in rooms and understanding not just what they were doing but why the architecture of their psychology made it inevitable.

She was already running scenarios. Not one scenario. Dozens. Testing each for plausibility, durability, and risk.

"The information has to be believable," she said. "Close enough to the truth that the person receiving it doesn't question it. Which means you need to tell me what the truth is."

The President looked at her for a long moment. Then he told her.

Cartwright did not move. Seymour folded his hands. Tamara's attention sharpened almost visibly. Rafi felt the familiar sensation of a room crossing an invisible threshold.

What he said took eleven minutes.

When he finished, none of them spoke for a while.

The silence afterward was not shock. It was calculation. Each of them was determining how the new information altered the map they had been using up to this point.

Outside — four hundred meters east, three floors above, in the warm golden dining room — the evening was ending. The dessert cart was completing its rounds. The last guests were finding their coats. Dixie's bass and Freeman's guitar were playing something quiet and final, the music that meant the night had given everything it had and was now, gently, releasing the room back to the city.

Viktor Selin, Dianne knew, was still at table seven.

She knew because she knew him now — knew the psychological profile well enough to know that a man at the threshold of threshold, a man who had been given a Sazerac that unlocked something he thought he'd sealed, a man who had heard I'd Rather Go Blind with three voices behind it and forgotten to perform not-feeling it — that man did not leave until the music stopped.

He was waiting, without knowing he was waiting, for permission to go.

Some people waited for information. Others waited for certainty. Viktor, increasingly, seemed to be waiting for something he could not yet name.

She would give it to him.

And when she did, he would carry something out of this building that would travel up whatever chain he belonged to, and that chain would lead — through pathways Rafi would follow, through frequencies Seymour would track, through the financial signatures of frightened money in a Liechtenstein account — to a name on a list of seven.

"All right," Dianne said.

She said it the way she always said the thing that meant they were committed — quietly, completely, with the full weight of a woman who understood exactly what she was agreeing to.

"We'll need a week," she said. "Thursday again. Same room, same table, same everything. I need him to come back because he wants to, not because he's been directed to. That means this week I give him the room and let him leave wanting more of it."

The strategy depended on desire. Coercion left traces. Genuine attachment often did not.

She paused.

“And I need to know which of the seven you’re most afraid of.” The President looked at her.

He was the kind of man who did not frighten easily. Which made what she saw move across his face — briefly, controlled, suppressed in under a second — more diagnostic than anything she’d seen in the dining room all evening.

There it was. Not fear exactly. But proximity to it. Close enough to matter.

“I’ll have Cartwright send you the file,” he said.

“I don’t want a file,” Dianne said. “I want you to tell me. Right now. In this room. Which one.”

A long moment.

The room seemed to contract around the silence. Not physically, but in the way important information alters the atmosphere before anyone speaks.

The President told her. She did not write it down. She did not need to.

She looked at the table for three seconds — the time it took to file the name beside everything she already knew, to begin building the psychological architecture the mission required, to understand the full dimensions of what they were walking back into.

Years of clinical work had taught her that names were rarely just names. They arrived carrying histories, patterns, blind spots, loyalties, and fears. This one arrived carrying all of them.

Then she looked up.

“We’ll be ready Thursday,” she said.

There was no hesitation in it. Whatever private reaction the name had produced had already been moved aside and filed for later examination. The operation came first.

The Corridor: 10:09 PM They walked back in the same order.

Dianne first. Rafi at her left shoulder. Tamara behind. Seymour at the rear. Halfway down the corridor Tamara said: "Are you going to tell us the name?" "Not yet," Dianne said.

"Why not yet?" "Because the name changes how you look at people," Dianne said. "And I need you to look at people the way you always look at people for one more week."

The answer satisfied no one completely. Which was part of the reason it was the correct answer.

Tamara was quiet for a moment.

"Is it someone in this corridor?" she asked. Dianne walked eleven steps before she answered. "No," she said.

Rafi exhaled — the smallest, most controlled exhale, barely a sound. But Dianne heard it and understood it and loved him for it, because it meant that what she had just said had mattered to him in a way that confirmed, if confirmation were needed, that Rafi Delacroix was the one piece of this architecture that was not a variable.

The reaction lasted less than a second. Most people would have missed it. Dianne missed very little.

Seymour said nothing.

He never said anything in the corridor. He used the walk the way he used the space between musical phrases — to process, to prepare, to arrive at the next thing completely ready.

Silence, for Seymour, was never empty. It was usually where the work was happening.

They reached the door. Dianne unlocked it.

The wine cellar received them — cool, dark, the bottles watching.

Above them the dining room was settling into its final quiet. The music softer now, the last conversations finding their natural conclusions, the evening doing what evenings at Miss Dianne's always did in their last hour.

Becoming something worth remembering.

The room had developed that quality surprisingly quickly. Some establishments spent decades trying to become memorable. This one seemed to have decided from the beginning that it would be.

The Dining Room: 10:14 PM She came through the kitchen. Straightened her silk. Found her face. She walked to table seven.

Selin looked up.

She sat across from him — not the way Tamara sat, with the warmth and the theater of it, but simply. Two people at the end of an evening.

"You stayed," she said.

"The music," he said. And then, after a moment: "And the room."

Dianne looked at her room. At the last candles. At the dessert cart returning to the kitchen. At Freeman's guitar resting on its stand while Freeman stood at the edge of the stage talking to Stephon in the easy, unhurried way of two musicians after a good night. At Dixie winding down her bass cable with the practiced economy of a woman who had done it ten thousand times.

At Seymour's hands on the keys, playing something that had no name, that existed only in this moment, in this room, on this particular Thursday in October.

"It does that," she said. "It makes you want to stay."

She let the silence sit between them comfortably — because she had built a room where silence was comfortable, and because comfortable silence was the most advanced intelligence asset she had ever deployed.

Then she said: "Come back next Thursday."

He looked at her — not the way he'd looked at the music, not the way he'd looked at Tamara, but differently. Directly. As though he were trying to read something and knew that what he found would matter.

"Why?" he asked.

Dianne considered him — the question beneath the question, the man beneath the performance, the threshold he was standing at without knowing it — and told him the truth.

"Because," she said, "this room has more to give you."

Viktor Selin looked at the table. At his glass. At the last of the music moving through the room like something alive.

"Thursday," he said. "Thursday," she said.

She rose. Touched the back of his chair as she passed — the briefest contact, the gesture of a host seeing a guest toward the door — and walked back into her room.

Golden. Quiet.

Full of the particular satisfaction of an evening that had been, by every measure the world above the tunnel could see, an extraordinary success.

Below the wine cellar, the amber light had returned to green.

In the kitchen, Antoine was plating nothing and cleaning everything and reviewing in his precise memory every detail of the evening that had not made it into anyone else's report. *At table four, Rafi sat alone with a glass of wine he had finally allowed himself to drink, his notebook open to a fresh left-hand page that he had not yet written on.* *He was thinking about the corridor — specifically about the eleven steps he had counted, walking back, between Dianne's answer and his exhale. Eleven steps. He had been counting without meaning to, which was the kind of thing his mind did when it was managing something it could not otherwise manage.* She had said: no. The name was not in this corridor. He had exhaled.

And she had heard it. He knew she had heard it — had seen the almost- imperceptible acknowledgment cross her face, the clinical notation of a woman who missed nothing, filed it, and kept walking. She had heard his relief and she had not asked him about it, which was the kindness. And she had looked at him, briefly, in the way she sometimes looked at him — as though she were reaching for something that was almost within reach and then choosing, for now, to leave it. He was on the left-hand page of the seventeenth notebook.

He wrote: Thursday, October. Tunnel. She said no. She looked at me. He considered the entry.

He added: Still approaching. Closer. He closed the notebook.

He ran the numbers — not the financial ones, which he would return to in the morning, but the human ones: the calculus of risk and loyalty and the eleven years of proximity to a woman who did not know yet that he had been her neighbor before he was her colleague, her friend before he was her analyst, the person who had held her story while she could not hold it herself. The person who had three houses down and then three blocks and then a table in her own dining room made himself present, always present, at the exact distance she needed, which was the distance he could bear. The numbers balanced.

For now.

He drank his wine.

End of Chapter Three

Chapter Four: The Distribution List

The name the President had given her was not a surprise. This was the worst kind of name to be given.

Surprises could be processed — filed in the category of unknown variables now resolved, integrated into the operational architecture without disturbing the existing structure. But a name that was not a surprise arrived with a history attached. With every interaction retroactively reexamined. With the particular vertigo of a woman who had spent thirty years reading people and was now required to account for the fact that this one had been reading her back.

Dianne sat in her office on the third floor — a room that appeared on no floor plan shared with any contractor, accessed through a door that presented itself as a wall panel in the private dining room — and did not sleep.

It was two-seventeen in the morning.

The restaurant breathed around her — the particular respiration of old brick settling into cold, the HVAC cycling down to its overnight register, the silence that was never quite silence in a building this age and this history.

She had come to know its sounds the way she knew the sounds of her own body. From the inside. Without having to think about it.

She had a legal pad in front of her. She had written nothing on it.

This was unusual. Dianne worked on paper — always, instinctively, because the physical act of writing engaged a different cognitive process than typing, and because paper could be destroyed in ways that servers could not. Her legal pads were her thinking. And her thinking was the most valuable and most protected thing she possessed.

But tonight the pad was blank.

Because the name the President had given her existed in a part of her mind where she was not yet ready to write it down.

She looked at it instead.

Turned it.

Examined it from the angles she would examine any subject — behavioral history, psychological profile, motivational architecture, the specific and particular way this person's childhood had built the adult who had then built the choices that had led to a device in a dining room floor and a distribution list of seven and a question that had no comfortable answer. She had known this person for a long time.

That was the only thing she needed to sit with before she could work. She sat with it until three o'clock.

Then she picked up her pen and began.

Friday: Rafi Rafi did not sleep either, but for different reasons.

He was in the restaurant's back office — a real office, on real floor plans, containing real financial records of a very successful Georgetown restaurant — with three screens running and a pot of coffee that had been excellent at midnight and was now something else entirely at two in the morning, and he did not care, because Rafi Delacroix had the quality of focus that makes food and sleep optional when something in the numbers was not right.

Something in the numbers was not right.

He had learned this quality in a neighborhood where the numbers were almost never right — where the gap between what a family earned and what a family needed was the first math a child learned, more reliable than anything in a textbook, and where reading that gap accurately was the difference between the decision that kept you and the decision that cost you. He had sat at his mother's kitchen table with a composition notebook — his first composition notebook, the one before the seventeen that contained Dianne — and taught himself, at nine years old, to follow money through the layered economy of a block in New Orleans where everything was connected and the connections told the story that the surface refused to tell.

He had been following money through layers ever since. The layers changed. The principle did not.

He had been following the Liechtenstein account since Tuesday and it had led him through Cyprus and then the Caymans and then a private bank in Singapore whose discretion was legendary and whose client list was a matter of considerable international speculation — to a structure he recognized.

Not the specific structure. The *type.* He had seen this architecture before — this precise combination of layering depth, cutout complexity, and what he thought of as operational patience, the willingness to build financial cover over years rather than months — in exactly one other context. A briefing, three years ago, in a room without windows, delivered by a woman who worked for a division of the agency that didn't use the agency's name.

The briefing had been about how a specific hostile foreign intelligence service funded its domestic operations.

The type matched.

Rafi stared at his screens and understood that the Liechtenstein account was not merely frightened money.

It was institutional money.

Money placed by an organization with a budget, a doctrine, a methodology refined over decades. Which meant that whoever on the distribution list was connected to it was not freelancing. They had been recruited. Developed.

Handled. For some duration Rafi could not yet determine.

He opened a fresh page in his notebook — the right-hand page, the operational page, not the left — and wrote at the top one word: *Duration.* Because duration was everything. Duration told you how deep the damage went, how much had already been passed, whether the operation was salvageable or whether Thursday was already compromised before it began. Duration was the question that could not be answered from the money alone — the money showed you the path but not the timeline, the structure but not the start date.

He would need to go further back.

He started following the money backward, the way he had learned to follow everything backward — with patience, with the full weight of his training and his childhood and the seventeen notebooks that had taught him that the most important information was always the information that arrived before the story officially began.

Friday: Seymour Seymour slept four hours and was back in the restaurant by six in the morning. He walked to the bandstand and sat at the piano.

He did not play.

He placed his hands on the keys the way he placed his hands on keys when he was thinking rather than performing — lightly, without pressure, the connection of familiarity rather than intention — and looked at Jerome's kit, which Jerome had left precisely as Jerome always left it: perfect, locked, unavailable to anyone who didn't know where the real components were.

Jerome had sent him the directional detector logs at two-seventeen in the morning. Seymour had read them at two-eighteen, which was the benefit of being a man who had trained himself to sleep in short, total increments and to wake fully rather than gradually. The logs contained the bearing data for the external receiver's two passes —

east on M Street, first pass at eight forty-nine, second pass at eight fifty-eight — and Jerome's annotation in the sparse technical shorthand he used for operational notes: *vehicle, not pedestrian. Speed consistent with slow roll. Same bearing both passes.

Second pass collected the burst.* A vehicle moving slowly east on M Street. Past the building.

Twice.

Seymour had gone back to sleep. He had thought about it for exactly the duration of time between wakefulness and sleep, which for him was brief, and when he woke at five-forty he had arrived at the piece Jerome had not yet had time to work out, because Jerome had been running the detector build and the disable and the clone simultaneously across the three weeks prior and had not had the bandwidth to run the pattern analysis Seymour had spent four hours doing in his sleep.

The vehicle.

He had the M Street camera data — which was not publicly available but was available to people with Jerome's clearance, which Jerome had given Seymour access to three months ago in precisely this kind of situation — and he had cross-referenced the two passes from last night against the same bearing on all eleven previous collection evenings. The same vehicle.

Not similar. The same.

He had the make and model from the plate capture on the third occurrence — a dark grey sedan of a specific year and specific manufacturer, registered to a consulting firm in Bethesda whose incorporation documents Rafi was currently examining from the back office, which was why Seymour had forwarded the plate data to Rafi at three AM without explanation and had received, at three forty-seven, a single reply: *I see it.* Rafi saw it.

Seymour sat at the piano and thought about what the vehicle meant.

A vehicle meant a driver. A driver on eleven specific Thursdays — the high- operational Thursdays, the Thursdays Jerome had identified as the collection schedule's preferred evenings — who knew enough to pass twice, slow, at the precise window when Jerome's floor tom said the beacon was transmitting. This was not Paul.

Paul was the physical collector — the man with the phone at the base of the kit, three seconds, short-range transfer. Paul collected what the baseboard device had stored.

The vehicle collected something different.

The vehicle was collecting the beacon's status transmission. Two separate collection mechanisms. Two separate chains.

The baseboard device transmitted to Paul's phone on a short-range physical protocol. The baseboard device also transmitted a beacon on a separate frequency to a vehicular receiver.

Two handlers. Two chains. Two separate pieces of an architecture designed so that no single point of failure could compromise the whole.

This was not one hostile actor. This was a structure.

Seymour pressed a single chord into the keys. Minor. Unresolved.

The sound of a problem that was larger than it had appeared. He covered the keyboard, stood, and went to find Dianne.

Friday: The Third Floor Office, 7:12 AM She had filled four pages of the legal pad by the time Seymour knocked — three soft taps, the knock he used when the information was urgent but not emergency.

The knock that said *I have something, take a moment if you need it.* "Come in," she said.

He came in and sat across from her desk and looked at the legal pad the way people looked at Dianne's legal pads when they understood what they represented.

"The vehicle has been there eleven times," he said. "Same plate. Same bearing. Same window. I have it from the camera data."

He set his phone on her desk. "Rafi is running the registration now."

She looked at the plate number.

"And it's not Paul's collection mechanism," she said. Not a question. She had already arrived at the two-chain architecture — he could see it in the stillness she used for conclusions rather than questions.

"Paul takes what the baseboard stores," Seymour said. "The vehicle receives the beacon. They're separate protocols. Separate handlers."

"Which means," Dianne said, "that whoever built this is running a redundant collection architecture. If Paul is caught, the beacon chain survives.

If the vehicle is identified, the physical collection chain survives."

"Yes."

"And Jerome's clone maintains the beacon. So the vehicle chain continues to believe the device is operational."

"Correct."

She turned her pen in her fingers. One rotation. Two. "When is our next wine delivery?" she said.

Seymour looked at her. "Today," he said. "Ten o'clock."

Friday: The Wine Delivery, 10:04 AM She watched from the bar.

She had positioned herself with a cup of coffee and the week's reservation book — physical, leather, another of her non-negotiable decisions — and watched the delivery team move through the dining room with the practiced efficiency of people who had done this enough times to stop seeing the room.

Three men. She knew all three. Had vetted all three. Had eaten lunch with Gerald, the distributor, a man who had been supplying serious Washington restaurants for thirty years and whose integrity was, to Dianne's professional assessment, not in question.

She watched the first man wheel the dolly through the service entrance.

The second — young, four weeks on the job, she had his file and found nothing. The third.

His name was Paul. He had been on this delivery route since they opened. He was fifty-three. Unremarkable in the way that made Dianne's attention sharpen rather than relax, because unremarkable was sometimes natural and sometimes constructed and she had spent thirty years learning to tell the difference.

He moved through the dining room. He paused at the bandstand.

It was a natural pause — the pause of a man who spent his working hours in functional spaces and found himself, each week, briefly in a room that was something else. He looked at Seymour's piano the way people looked at things they found beautiful but had no words for.

Three seconds.

She watched his right hand.

His right hand, at his side, was holding a phone. Routine. Everyone held their phone. It meant nothing.

But the angle of it — the precise, specific angle at which the phone's lower edge was oriented toward the base of Jerome's kit — was not routine.

It was exact.

It was the angle of a man who had been told, with technical precision, the location of a device and the orientation required for a three-second short- range transfer.

He didn't look at the phone. He didn't look at the kit.

He looked at the piano, with the expression of a man appreciating something beautiful, and his right hand stayed exactly where it was for exactly three seconds, and then he moved on toward the wine cellar with his dolly and his unremarkable face and his phone in his pocket that now contained three weeks of everything Miss Dianne's Jazz and Blues Kitchen had heard.

Dianne did not move.

She turned a page in the reservation book.

She wrote, in the margin of Thursday's reservation page, in handwriting only she could read: *Paul. 10:07. Confirmed.* Then she poured what remained of her coffee and drank it and looked at her dining room — her beautiful, golden, carefully engineered dining room — and added one more piece to the architecture she had been building since three o'clock in the morning.

Paul was not the name the President had given her. Paul was the mechanism.

Which meant the name the President had given her had sent Paul here.

Which meant the name the President had given her had known about the construction schedule, the technical specifications, the array inside Jerome's kit — She stopped.

She set down her coffee cup.

She picked it up again because she needed something to hold.

The name the President had given her had known about Jerome's kit. The design of Jerome's kit was known to exactly four people in the world — Jerome, Seymour, the agency technician who had approved the specs, and the person on the distribution list who had oversight of technical operations.

The distribution list had seven names. She ran them.

She arrived at the intersection of technical oversight and institutional money and the particular psychological profile of someone who had been watching her build this operation from the inside.

She arrived at the name the President had given her.

She arrived at it from a different direction than she'd arrived at it the night before.

It was the same name.

The fact that it was the same name from a different direction was the certainty the President had said he needed.

She had it.

Friday Afternoon: The Assembly They met at two o'clock in the private dining room. Dianne, Tamara, Rafi, Seymour.

No Antoine yet. Antoine would be briefed on what he needed for Thursday and nothing beyond it, because operational security now required that everyone know only the layer they were working in.

Dianne stood.

She never sat when she was running a briefing.

She told them about Paul — the angle of the phone, the three seconds, the confirmation.

She told them about the financial architecture Rafi had traced — the Liechtenstein account, the institutional signature, the duration question.

She looked at Rafi.

"How far back?" she asked.

"The account structure traces to eighteen months before our operational brief was written," Rafi said. "They weren't responding to us. They were anticipating us."

He paused, and the pause carried the weight of what that meant. "Someone told them this operation was being planned before it had a name."

The room absorbed this.

"And the name," Tamara said.

She said it quietly. To Dianne specifically. The way you say something to a person you have known long enough to understand what it costs them.

Dianne told them the name.

The private dining room was very quiet.

Seymour looked at the table. His hands, which were almost never still, were still.

Tamara's face did something brief and private and then composed itself. Rafi looked at Dianne for a long moment.

"You're sure," he said. Not a challenge. The question of a man who needed to hear the architecture before he could carry it.

"I arrived at the same name from three independent directions," Dianne said. "Psychological profile, technical access, and the money. Yes. I'm sure."

A silence that had the texture of grief, briefly. Then everyone in the room did what the room required — set it aside, filed it where it would be tended to later, in private, at a time when the operation had no need of their feelings about it.

"All right," Tamara said.

She said it the way Dianne had said *all right* in the tunnel — completely, with the full weight of a woman who understood what she was agreeing to.

"Tell us Thursday," she said.

The Architecture of Thursday Dianne told them Thursday.

She told it from the foundation up, every element in its place, every contingency accounted for before anyone asked. The psychological operation she had designed overnight was the most intricate she had ever built, because it required simultaneous management of four separate objectives: turning Selin, feeding him the false intelligence, managing the collection by Paul, and — beneath all of it, invisible to everyone except the people in this room — sending a message to the name the President had given her.

Not a message that would be recognized as a message. Not yet.

A message that would only be understood in its full meaning after Thursday. The kind that Dianne specialized in — the ones that arrived after the fact, that revealed themselves slowly, that told a person not what you knew but that you had always known. The most destabilizing communication a clinical forensic psychologist could send to a person operating on the assumption that their cover was intact.

She outlined the false intelligence — the specific, verifiable, exquisitely crafted lie the President had approved, that Rafi had built the financial scaffolding for, that Seymour would embed in a conversation in the acoustic space his band had calibrated.

She outlined Tamara's role — which was, as always, to be the room. To make Selin feel what he needed to feel. To move the evening to the moment when Dianne could deliver the intelligence in a way

Selin would absorb completely, genuinely, in the neurological register of real information rather than performance.

She outlined Seymour's role — the songs, the frequencies, the specific acoustic architecture of two conversations that needed to happen simultaneously without either party aware of the other.

She outlined Rafi's role — table four, notebook, financial surveillance of every instrument in the room, and the specific signal he would give at the moment the collection happened.

She outlined what happened after Thursday. When she finished, the room was quiet.

Then Tamara said: "What's the third song?" Dianne looked at her.

"*A Change Is Gonna Come,*" Dianne said. Tamara was quiet for a moment.

"Sam Cooke," she said.

"Yes."

"You're sending a message with the third song."

"I'm sending several," Dianne said. "Thursday is full of them."

Thursday Minus Six Days The week moved with the quality of time that operational weeks always have — compressed in the foreground, endless in the background. The days passing quickly in the work and slowly in the waiting the work required.

Dianne profiled.

Forty hours across six days reviewing everything she had on the name — behavioral history, financial signatures, professional record, the interpersonal patterns that were visible in retrospect as the patterns of a person living two lives simultaneously. She built the psychological architecture of the person she was dealing with the way she built all her profiles: from the outside in, from behavior to motive to the specific wound or conviction or fear that had made the behavior possible.

What she found was not a monster.

This was always the difficulty with the ones who weren't monsters. They were comprehensible. Which made them harder in ways that pure antagonism was not. She understood the journey. She could trace the decision points, the moments where the road forked and this person had taken the turn that led, eventually, to Paul and his phone and three seconds at the base of Jerome Park's drum kit. Understanding was not forgiveness.

She had made peace with that early in her career.

But it informed the operation. Because a person who could be understood could be predicted. And a person who could be predicted could be positioned.

Thursday, she was going to position this person very precisely.

Rafi traced the money forward.

He was looking for the endpoint — the account or entity that the intelligence eventually reached, the financial fingerprint of the institutional handler. This was the piece the President needed beyond the name, because a foreign intelligence service running an asset inside a Presidential operation required a diplomatic response targeted at exactly the right level.

The money was patient and the money was deep and the money was, as all seriously constructed financial architecture eventually is, imperfect.

He found the imperfection on Wednesday morning at four forty-seven — a transaction made sixteen months ago from a subsidiary of a subsidiary of a European holding company to a research foundation in Washington that was legitimate, respected, and had on its advisory board three names Rafi recognized from his briefing files.

One of those names had diplomatic immunity.

He photographed the screen, locked his notebook in the office safe, and went home to sleep for the first time in thirty-six hours.

Seymour rehearsed.

Not the band. The band didn't need rehearsal in the conventional sense, because the band was always ready, because musicians of this caliber were always either playing or about to play with no meaningful distinction between the states.

He rehearsed the acoustic geometry of Thursday.

He sat at the piano in the empty dining room and played through the set, calibrating the frequencies, adjusting the temperatures, finding the specific musical environment in which two simultaneous conversations could occur in complete acoustic privacy from each other.

He played *A Change Is Gonna Come* alone in the room at eleven o'clock on Wednesday night.

He played it slowly. With the full weight of everything Sam Cooke had put in it and everything the years since had added to it. The empty dining room received it the way the room received everything Seymour gave it — completely, without judgment, with the pure attentiveness of a space built for exactly this.

When he finished he sat at the piano for a while in the dark.

He was tired.

This was not something Seymour Emerson admitted often or easily — the fatigue of a man managing two simultaneous and fully demanding operations, one musical and one otherwise, each of which required everything he had and neither of which was willing to accept less. The musical operation he could sustain indefinitely. He had been sustaining it since he was six years old. The other one — the weight of what he knew, of what the room was carrying, of what the Thursday ahead required — had its own metabolic cost, and he was not too proud to acknowledge it in the dark, alone, with no one to manage the acknowledgment for.

He was frustrated.

The name Dianne was carrying — the name she had not yet given them from the President, the name she needed them not to know for one more week — was a weight he was carrying blind. He could feel its shape from the outside. He had his suspicions. He had not acted on his suspicions because Dianne had asked him not to, and because Dianne's operational instincts were the finest he had worked beside, and because trust, in a unit of this kind, was the only currency that could not be replaced once spent.

But he was frustrated.

And so he was sitting at the piano in the empty dining room at eleven-seventeen on a Wednesday night, running through the week's request book — the leather binder from the host stand, which Roy Baptiste had left on the piano lid per Seymour's standing Wednesday instruction — reviewing which requests were playable on Thursday, which needed to wait, which needed to be declined with the particular grace the room's standards required.

He turned the pages.

Seventeen cards this week. Mostly familiar territory. *Fever.* *Dock of the Bay.* Three separate requests for *Harvest Moon*, which was the song most often requested by people who had heard it once and needed to hear it again.

At Last. A request for *St. James Infirmary* written in the handwriting of the Norwegian attaché, which Seymour noted and set aside with the satisfaction of a man whose regulars had excellent taste.

He turned to the sixteenth card. He stopped.

He read it again.

Who's Keeping Watch of My Old Lady. He sat with the card for a moment.

The handwriting was neat. Block capitals, evenly spaced — the handwriting of someone writing carefully rather than naturally, which was the first thing.

The second thing was the song itself.

He knew it. Of course he knew it — Seymour Emerson knew every song that had ever been recorded in every genre that had ever produced a song worth recording, which was a consequence of forty years of obsessive, systematic listening that had produced in him a musical memory as complete and cross-indexed as any archive. The song was a late-period Southern rock track — 1974, a regional pressing from a Muscle Shoals session that had never found national distribution, recorded by a band whose name had not survived the decade, whose catalog was known only to the kind of collectors who drove six hours to a barn sale for the possibility of finding exactly this record in a milk crate. It was not a song that appeared in request books.

It was not a song that guests of Miss Dianne's Jazz and Blues Kitchen would know. The room's demographic — diplomatic corps, former Cabinet officials, the Georgetown professional community, the serious music lovers who had found their Thursday and claimed it — ran to Etta James and Sam Cooke and Billie Holiday and the jazz standards. On the occasional adventurous evening, Bill Withers. On the very rare Thursday when the room was feeling its Southern roots,

Fats Domino or Little Richard, and always with a request framing that acknowledged the departure: *I know this is unusual, but—* This card had no such framing. It simply named the song.

As though the person writing it knew it would be known. Seymour turned the card over.

Nothing on the back.

He looked at the seating number Roy had written in the upper corner of the card in the standard notational shorthand he used when he collected them from the tables: *T-12*. Table twelve. The corner table on the south wall, the one the room's operational architecture put furthest from the bandstand and closest to the street-side windows.

He had not looked at table twelve closely tonight.

He thought about this.

He thought about the vehicle on M Street. The dark grey sedan. The eleven evenings. The window between eight forty-seven and nine-oh-one.

He thought about the request arriving on a Wednesday — not a Thursday, not a service evening, but a Wednesday, which meant the card had been delivered to the host stand during lunch service, which the restaurant ran on a reduced capacity three days a week, which was not a high-operational window by any definition, which was exactly the kind of window in which someone who understood the operational calendar would choose to deliver a message they did not want received in a high-operational environment.

Not a request.

A message.

He sat at the piano and turned the card in his hands and thought about what a 1974 Southern rock song that no civilian guest of this dining room would know existed was doing in the request book of Miss Dianne's Jazz and Blues Kitchen.

He thought about the title.

Who's Keeping Watch of My Old Lady. He thought about it for a long time.

Who's keeping watch.

Of my old lady.

He set the card on the piano lid.

He placed his hands on the keys without pressing them.

He thought: it is not a song request. It is a question. Addressed to this room. From someone who knows what this room is and who is in it.

He thought: *who's keeping watch* — surveillance acknowledgment. They know they're being watched. They are telling us they know.

He thought: *of my old lady* — which in the argot of the era the song came from meant a woman. A specific woman. A woman of significance. The kind of phrase a handler used for an asset. Or the kind of phrase an asset used for a handler.

Or — and this was the thought that arrived last and stayed — the kind of phrase someone used for a person they were protecting.

He thought about the name Dianne was carrying. He thought about the distribution list of seven.

He thought about the vehicle on M Street. He picked up his phone.

He called Jerome.

Jerome answered on the second ring, which told Seymour he had not been asleep, which told Seymour that Jerome had also been thinking about the week ahead in the specific and sleepless way of a systems engineer who does not fully power down until the operation he is running reaches resolution.

"Wednesday lunch service," Seymour said. "Table twelve. Who was seated."

He heard Jerome at a keyboard. Six seconds.

"A single diner," Jerome said. "Reservation under a corporate account. The Listener logged a vocal signature for the table. Let me pull the classification."

Eight more seconds. Jerome said: "Seymour."

"Yes."

"The vocal signature at table twelve on Wednesday lunch matches a signature in the archive."

A pause. "It matches a signature from forty-one evenings of Thursday service. Not a guest signature. A service signature."

Seymour was very still.

"Which service position?" he said. Jerome told him.

Seymour sat at the piano for exactly four seconds.

"Don't call anyone else tonight," he said. "I'll be at the building at six AM."

He hung up.

He looked at the request card on the piano lid. Who's Keeping Watch of My Old Lady.

He thought about the person Jerome had just named.

He thought about the service position — the specific and unremarkable and entirely expected place in the room's weekly operation where a person could be present on forty-one Thursday evenings and forty-one Saturday lunches and forty-one Wednesday deliveries without anyone, including Seymour Emerson, looking twice.

He thought: *not Paul.* Not the vehicle.

Someone else. A third chain.

He thought: *the architecture is deeper than we understood.* He thought: *Dianne needs to know this tonight.* He covered the keys.

He left the request card on the piano lid. He did not call Dianne.

He drove to her building three blocks away and rang the bell and stood on the step in the October cold and waited, because some information was too consequential for a phone and some conversations needed to happen in person and some nights the operation did not allow for the formality of a reasonable hour.

She answered in forty-five seconds, which told him she had not been asleep either.

She looked at him.

He held up the card.

She read it.

She was quiet for three seconds. “Come in,” she said.

Wednesday Night: The Third Chain The conversation took forty minutes.

At the end of it they had three things they had not had at the beginning.

The first: a name. Not the name from the President’s distribution list — a different name, a name that existed in a different layer of the architecture, a name that connected the service position Jerome had identified to a presence that had been in the building not for forty-one Thursdays but for every single service day since before they opened — because the service position had been in place since the renovation, since before the first table was set and the first candle lit and the first guest arrived expecting dinner and found something more layered than dinner.

The second: an understanding of what *Who's Keeping Watch of My Old Lady* actually meant in the context of this room and this operation.

It was not a warning.

Dianne had known this within thirty seconds of reading the card, because warning communications from hostile actors did not quote 1974 Southern rock sessions from Muscle Shoals that had never achieved national distribution.

Warning communications were constructed to be legible. This was constructed to be found only by someone who already knew what they were looking for.

Which meant it was not addressed to Seymour. It was addressed to her.

Someone in the building — someone in the service position Jerome had identified — was asking Dianne Montague a question. Directly. In a language designed to pass through every filter except hers and Seymour's.

Who's keeping watch of my old lady — not surveillance language. Not asset language.

Protection language.

A person asking whether the woman they were protecting was being watched — not by the operation, but by the people the operation was designed to expose.

Seymour had understood this thirty seconds after Dianne. The third thing: a decision.

They would not pull the service position. They would not alter anything.

They would let the Wednesday lunch diner sit at table twelve next week and the week after and as many weeks as the operation required, and they would let the request card sit in the binder, and on Thursday Seymour would play three notes of *Who's Keeping Watch of My Old Lady* in the opening bars of *Autumn Leaves* — transposed, brief, unremarkable to anyone who did not know what they were hearing — and the person in the service position would hear the acknowledgment and would know that the room knew and that the room was not a threat and that the protection, whatever form it had been taking and for however long it had been running, was now operating in concert rather than in parallel.

Because the third chain was not a hostile chain. It was the opposite.

They did not yet know who it was protecting her from. But they knew it was protecting her.

And in a room full of things they did not fully understand, a room in which the device in the baseboard had listened since opening night and the vehicle on M Street had collected eleven Thursdays of heartbeats and the distribution list held a name the President had whispered in a spare room at the end of a four-hundred-meter tunnel — in that room, a piece of the architecture that was on their side rather than against it was not a complication.

It was a gift.

Seymour drove home at two in the morning. He slept four hours.

He arrived at the building at six, as he had said. Jerome was already there.

They sat in the basement rehearsal room and Jerome played him the vocal signature match and Seymour listened to it three times and said nothing until he had listened to it three times and then said: "All right."

Just that. All right.

The way you say it when something you have been carrying alone for longer than you realized has been seen by someone else, and the seeing changes the weight of it, and you are not yet ready to talk about what that means but you are ready to stop carrying it the way you've been carrying it. "All right," Seymour said.

He covered the piano.

He went upstairs to wait for Thursday.

End of Chapter Four

Chapter Five: Thursday Returns

The reservation said eight o'clock. He arrived at seven fifty-one.

Two minutes earlier than the first Thursday. Dianne noted it from the landing and added it to the profile without changing her expression. A man who had come seven minutes early on his first visit and two minutes earlier on his second was a man whose relationship with this room was deepening. The overcorrection was smaller because the need to appear casual had diminished.

He was beginning to feel he belonged here. Good.

That was the most dangerous thing she could give him.

She watched him settle into table seven with the ease of a man returning to something he has decided to trust, and she understood that the work of the past week — the Sazerac, the music, the three voices behind her on *I'd Rather Go Blind*, the comfortable silence at the end of the evening, the card in his pocket — had done exactly what it was designed to do.

He had come back because he wanted to.

Which meant he would hear what she needed him to hear, and he would believe it, and he would carry it out of this building without knowing he was carrying it, and the chain it traveled up would illuminate, like a wire made suddenly live, the name she already knew.

She descended at eight o'clock.

The room was full.

Not the same configuration as last Thursday — Dianne never repeated the seating configuration exactly, because patterns were information and information given freely was information wasted. Tonight the diplomatic corps was represented by four delegations rather than three. The former Secretary of State had come back, which she had expected. A new face at table nine — a woman she had been briefed on, a senior official from a European ministry with relevant oversight responsibilities, placed at table nine because of what table nine's acoustic relationship to table seven would allow. Rafi was at table four.

He had arrived at seven forty-five, which was earlier than his usual eight o'clock, because tonight his role began earlier. His notebook was open. His Meursault was poured. His three screens of financial surveillance were running on the laptop that presented itself as the kind of thing a man might bring to dinner if he were the kind of man who worked through dinner, which Rafi was, which made the laptop unremarkable.

He looked at the room.

He looked at the lot behind the building, which he could not see from here but could feel the way you feel the presence of something you have committed to — the ground next to the thing he loved, patient and cleared and waiting.

He opened his notebook to a fresh page.

The band arrived in their particular order.

Seymour first. Always Seymour first, because the bandstand was his, because the room's operational architecture began when his hands found the piano. He adjusted the bench. He ran the chord that was also a briefing.

We are live. We are recording. All systems are active. Tonight is different from every other night. Conduct yourselves accordingly. Jerome behind him, assembling the kit with the focused economy of a man for whom setup was also calibration — every piece placed with intention, the display inside the floor tom glowing its quiet confirmation that the array was running and the storage device in the bandstand was collecting and Paul would come on his schedule to collect from the storage device, and tonight when Paul came the signal would go to Rafi's notebook and from Rafi's notebook to Dianne.

Stephon at the Hammond, the B3 warming up with the low hum of an instrument that needed time to become itself— like a singer clearing the voice, like a mind shaking off sleep, the Leslie beginning its slow rotation that would build, over the next twenty minutes, to its full operatic warmth.

Celeste with her trumpet. Marcus at the edge of the stage, watching the room in the behavioral linguist's way — reading not words but the grammar of bodies, the syntax of how people positioned themselves relative to each other and what that positioning said about the power and the fear and the desire moving through the room beneath the dinner conversation.

Freeman on his stool. Guitar tonight, and the violin case open at his feet because Seymour had told him, without telling him, that tonight would need the violin before it was over. Freeman had looked at the case and nodded. That was the whole conversation.

Dixie at the upright bass. She plucked one string — a single note, low and resonant, that traveled through the floor of the bandstand and into the floor of the dining room and was felt rather than heard by the guests nearest the stage. A tuning note. Also a presence note. *I am here. The ground is here. Whatever happens, the foundation holds.* In the service corridor, Marcus Tureaud had his trumpet case open behind the linen station. Solange Arceneaux had positioned her trombone case beside the service bar in the specific location she always used on the nights when Dixieland was possible. Roy Baptiste had his clarinet case under the host stand.

They were all of them, in both of their capacities, ready.

Tamara found Selin at eight-seventeen.

She came to his table the way she always came to his table — with the warmth that was genuine and the attention that was total and the particular quality of focus that made every person she directed it toward feel temporarily, and not entirely incorrectly, that they were the most interesting person in the room.

She sat across from him. "You came back," she said.

"You said to come back on Thursday," he said.

"I say that to many people," she said. "Not everyone listens."

"I listened," he said.

She looked at him the way she looked at people when she was reading them at full depth rather than social depth — the theater training, the intelligence training, the thirty years of being in rooms where the surface and the substance were different things and her job was to know which was which.

He was more relaxed than last Thursday.

Not significantly. Not carelessly. A trained man's relaxation, which was still performance but was performance of a lower order than what he'd arrived with seven days ago. The room had already done some of the work.

She ordered him another Sazerac without asking. He noticed.

He said nothing.

He accepted it when it came with the grace of a man accepting something he has decided to let himself want.

"Tell me," Tamara said, with the ease of a woman who had all evening, "how you found us."

And Selin — who had been told how he'd found them, who had a cover story for how he'd found them that was plausible and complete — paused for a fraction of a second longer than the cover story required.

She filed it.

In the kitchen, Antoine was plating the third course with the focused precision of a man who took both of his jobs equally seriously.

He knew tonight was different because Dianne had told him it was different, which was the only information he needed. She had told him the fifth course would go to table seven before any other table, which meant the timeline was accelerating at the fifth course. Which meant whatever needed to happen would happen between the fifth course and the dessert cart.

He plated.

He waited.

He was, in his own estimation, very good at both.

The first song came at nine o'clock.

Dianne stepped onto the stage in ivory silk — the same ivory silk she always wore on Thursdays, because consistency was part of the room's architecture, because Selin needed to feel that this Thursday was another Thursday in a series of Thursdays that belonged to him, that this room gave itself to him on this night in this way reliably and would go on doing so.

She stood at the microphone.

Behind her, the three took their places without announcement.

Freeman with his guitar. Dixie at her bass, bow down, voice ready. Tamara at the edge of the stage — she had returned from Selin's table with the ease of a woman who had simply been doing her job and was now doing her other job, the two indistinguishable from any angle except the one that mattered.

Seymour played the opening of *I'd Rather Go Blind.* The room went still.

Dianne sang.

She sang it the way she always sang it — with the excavator's honesty, the total commitment of a woman who understood that a song was only as true as the person singing it was willing to be. Freeman's harmony arrived on the second verse. Dixie's foundation came in underneath. Tamara filled the space that only Tamara could fill.

At table seven, Viktor Selin stopped performing relaxation and simply sat.

The mask required active maintenance and the song had reached the mechanism that maintained it and interrupted the signal.

Dianne noted it from the stage. She filed it.

She held the last note until the room could bear it and then one beat longer. The applause began in the chest.

The intelligence was delivered at ten twenty-two.

This was Dianne's moment — the one she had designed across forty hours of profiling and one night of sleeplessness and the full weight of thirty years of clinical precision deployed in service of a single evening's work.

She had come to table seven after the first song, as naturally as a woman who owned the room might come to greet a guest she was pleased to see. She had sat across from Selin with the easy warmth of someone who had made a decision about him — which she had, though not the decision he understood — and they had talked about the music and the room and the particular quality of Washington in

October, which was a topic she had chosen because it was pleasant and because pleasant conversation was the acoustic cover for what was actually happening.

She watched him.

She watched the microexpressions, the breathing patterns, the small neurological tells that existed below the level of conscious control — the signs of a man who was, as she had assessed since week three of watching him, not the architect of whatever was moving through Washington's diplomatic channels but the messenger. The unwitting messenger. A man under pressure he had not anticipated, carrying information he did not fully understand, for people he had begun, she now believed, to fear.

She gave him the intelligence at ten twenty-two.

She did not hand him a document. She did not say anything that would have sounded, to anyone overhearing it, like intelligence. She embedded it in a conversation about the wine program — about a specific bottle, a specific provenance, a specific detail that was the false intelligence dressed as the kind of incidental knowledge that a woman who ran a serious restaurant might possess and share with a guest she trusted.

It took forty-seven seconds.

Selin received it the way she had designed for him to receive it — without recognizing it as intelligence, which was the only way that mattered. It landed in him the way real information lands: not as a briefing but as a texture, something that would surface later in a report that would not feel like a report because he would not remember receiving it as reportable.

Forty-seven seconds.

Thirty years of training.

One operation.

She picked up her wine glass and said something pleasant about the second half of the evening, and Selin smiled the third real smile she had counted from him, and she excused herself and walked back toward the bar.

At table four, Rafi's right hand moved almost imperceptibly. She had what she needed.

Paul arrived at eleven-oh-four.

He came in through the service entrance with the routine confidence of a man who had been doing this long enough that the building no longer noticed him — which was exactly what he needed the building to believe, and exactly what the building was prepared to let him believe tonight, on this specific visit, for the last time.

He moved through the kitchen. Nodded to Antoine. Headed toward the bandstand with the unhurried movement of a man taking the most direct route between two points, which happened to pass through the dining room, which happened to offer a brief view of a piano he had always found beautiful.

He paused at the bandstand. He looked at the piano.

His right hand, at his side, held his phone at the precise angle. Three seconds.

At table four, Rafi's notebook opened. He wrote three words in the margin and closed it again.

At the bar, Dianne saw the notebook open and close. She set down her glass.

The intelligence had been collected.

It was moving now — up through Paul to whoever Paul reported to, up through that chain to the name she had been given in the tunnel seven days ago, up through that name to the institutional handler whose financial signature Rafi had traced to a European holding company with a diplomatic advisory board.

It was moving.

And they would follow it every step of the way.

The second song came at ten o'clock — it had come before the intelligence, before Paul, in the proper order of the evening, because the evening had to feel like every other Thursday or it was not the room she had built — and it was *Got My Mojo Working,* because it was always *Got My Mojo Working* at ten o'clock on a Thursday, because this was a house with its own rhythms and those rhythms did not bend for operations.

Stephon's Hammond engaged fully. The Leslie opened up. The room felt it in the chest.

Freeman pulled his harmonica. Played eight bars of pure joy walking toward the front of the stage — the sound of a man who had started in a Pentecostal church in Shreveport at four years old and had never once lost the thread back to that room, that music, that particular and irreplaceable conviction that what was happening was real and mattered and deserved the whole body. Tamara was on the floor before the first chorus ended.

James appeared from the service corridor.

They found each other the way they always found each other — by rhythm, by instinct, by the shared understanding of two people for whom movement was a first language.

And tonight there was something else.

At a signal only the band could read — a specific rhythmic figure Jerome played that meant *now, if you're ready* — Marcus Tureaud walked out of the service corridor with his trumpet at his lips, already playing, the sound arriving in the room a half-second before anyone understood where it was coming from.

Solange Arceneaux followed with her trombone, the slide moving with the easy authority of a woman who had been doing this since before she knew what to call it.

Roy Baptiste was last, his clarinet finding the high obligato line that wove above everything else the way starlings move — individually free, collectively inevitable.

The room understood what was happening a few seconds after it had already happened, which is the only way a transformation of this kind works.

The jazz quartet had become a seven-piece Dixieland band.

Miss Dianne's Jazz and Blues Kitchen had become New Orleans. The former Secretary of State stood up from his table.

He did not dance — he was not, had never been, a dancer — but he stood, which was its own kind of statement, which was the body's honest response to music that does not request your participation but simply assumes it.

At table seven, Viktor Selin was on his feet.

He was smiling a smile that Dianne, from across the room, classified immediately and precisely: the smile of a man who has stopped calculating. Who has, for the duration of this music in this room on this Thursday in October, simply surrendered to the fact of joy.

She let him have it.

She had built this room to give people exactly this.

And the operation needed him loose and warm and trusting for what was about to come.

The third song came at eleven.

This was *A Change Is Gonna Come.* Seymour announced it the way he announced things that mattered — not with words but with the quality of the silence he let fall before his hands found the keys. A specific silence. The silence of a man who has chosen this song carefully and is acknowledging the weight of the choice before he makes it.

The dining room felt the silence and paid attention.

Stephon moved from the Hammond to the piano bench beside Seymour — the two keyboards side by side, the two men finding their respective registers the way they always found them, Seymour taking the melody and Stephon taking the orchestral depth beneath it, the sound between them larger than either could have produced alone.

Freeman reached for the violin.

He drew the bow across the strings once — a single long note, open and clear, the sound of something being said plainly — and then settled into the arrangement Seymour had built, the violin taking the countermelody that wove around Dianne's voice the way the original brass arrangement had woven around Cooke's, honoring the tradition while making something new of it.

Dianne stepped to the microphone. She looked at her room.

She found, without appearing to find, the face she was looking for.

Not Selin. Not tonight. Tonight there was another face she needed to find — the face of the person the President had named, who was in this room as they were always in this room on Thursday evenings, whose presence here had been as unremarkable as the candles and the music and the dessert cart until it was not.

She found the face.

She held it for less than a second — the duration of a breath, the duration of a decision — and then let her gaze move on in the natural way of a woman looking at her room.

But she had found it.

And the person whose face she had found would not have been able to say, precisely, why the look from across the room had felt different from every other Thursday. Would not have been able to articulate what had changed in the room's temperature when Dianne Montague's eyes moved across their face with the easy ownership of a woman in her own dining room.

Would not have been able to explain the feeling. But would feel it.

That was the message. Not the song, not the words of it — though the words were chosen and the words were true and *a change is gonna come* meant exactly what it said. The message was the look. Three hundred milliseconds of eye contact from a woman who knew. Dianne sang.

I was born by the river, in a little tent.

Behind her, Tamara's voice arrived — not with the harmonic warmth of *Harvest Moon*, not with the driving support of *Got My Mojo Working*, but with something older and more serious. The voice of a woman who understood what the song required and gave it everything the requirement demanded.

Freeman's violin wove around both of them. Dixie's voice came in on the second verse — the deep foundation, the thing beneath the thing, the ground holding.

The three backup singers and the violin and the two pianos and Dixie's bass and Jerome's brushes on the ride cymbal built the song the way a river builds its current — not by force but by accumulation, each element adding to what was already there until the whole thing was moving with a power that had nothing to do with volume and everything to do with truth.

The room was completely still.

Viktor Selin, at table seven, had his eyes closed.

The former Secretary of State had sat back down and was looking at the floor in the way people look at the floor when they are experiencing something they want to be private about.

At table four, Rafi had not opened his notebook in twenty minutes. He was looking at the stage with the expression he wore when he allowed himself to be exactly where he was — the composed, private face of a man who had loved these women since before he understood what love required of him, who had spent eleven years carrying what they could not carry themselves, who had built a fifteen-volume document of perfect financial architecture as an act of love so complete it presented as a business plan. He was looking at Dianne on the stage.

He was remembering a specific Thursday — the third Thursday they had been open, six weeks into the operation and six weeks into the restaurant and six weeks into the experience of sitting at this table watching this woman stand at that microphone — when she had sung *Unforgettable* and in the second verse had closed her eyes and had not opened them again until the last note, and he had written in the left-hand page of the twelfth notebook, in the small private handwriting, a single word: *soon.* He had been wrong that Thursday. Soon had not meant what he thought it meant then. But he had kept writing it, in the months and the Thursdays that followed, because it was the most honest word available and because the notebooks were where he was most honest, and because *soon* was the word that kept the waiting from becoming something harder than waiting.

He was looking at Dianne on the stage.

He was thinking about a photograph on a round table twelve steps below — two girls on a porch in New Orleans, one pointing, one laughing, and the handwriting on the white Polaroid border that had faded while the image had not, and his copy of the same photograph in a frame on his desk at home that he had never once considered moving.

He was thinking about the lot behind the building, cleared and fenced and patient.

He was thinking about the seventeenth notebook in his inside pocket. He was thinking about the footnote on the last page of Volume Fifteen. He was thinking: *not yet.* He was thinking: *but the song is right. A change is gonna come.* He was thinking: *I have been waiting since I was nine years old. I can wait a little longer.* He was thinking: *soon.* Dianne held the last note of *A Change Is Gonna Come* the way she held all last notes — past the comfortable length, into the honest length, the place where the sound became something more than sound and the room became something more than a room and the evening became what the best evenings always become: proof that what is real and what is beautiful are not, despite everything Washington would have you believe, mutually exclusive. The note resolved.

The room held the silence for a moment.

Then it returned to itself — slowly, the way you return from something that has taken you somewhere real, with the particular tenderness of a room that has been changed by what it just contained.

The applause was the kind that doesn't start all at once. It started in one corner — the Norwegian attaché, who had been here every Thursday since the first time Tamara had curtsied at him and who had long since stopped pretending he came for the food — and spread the way true things spread, from person to person, until the room was fully in it.

Freeman lowered his violin.

He pressed his right hand briefly to his chest, the gesture of a man from Shreveport who learned before he learned anything else that music of this kind requires gratitude as well as technique.

Tamara stepped down from the edge of the stage with the ease of a woman returning from one country to another, both of which she inhabited fluently.

Dixie set her bow down across the strings of the bass and let out a slow breath that was also a thank you.

Seymour lifted his hands from the keys and placed them in his lap and was still for a moment in the way he was still after the songs that had demanded everything — not depleted, but complete. A man who had given what was asked and found that giving it had not diminished him.

Across the room, at the table Dianne had placed them at for exactly these sightlines, the person whose name the President had given her sat with a glass of wine and a face that was, to any casual observer, simply the face of someone who had just experienced something moving in a room full of music.

To Dianne it was something else.

She read it the way she read everything — precisely, without editorial, the clinical observation of a fact that existed below the performance of the face.

The face of a person who had just received a message they could not have articulated but could not unfeel.

The message had landed.

The week that followed would confirm it. The false intelligence would move up through Paul's phone, up through the chain, to the institutional handler whose financial fingerprint Rafi had traced to a European holding company on a Wednesday morning at four forty-seven. It would surface in a form that Seymour would detect and Jerome would record and Rafi would trace and that Cartwright's people, watching from table eleven, would confirm was exactly what the President had needed it to be.

Certainty.

The operation would close.

The name would no longer be only the President's to carry. But all of that was next week.

Tonight there was still the dessert cart.

It arrived when the room had settled into itself — when the evening had found its final rhythm and no one was in any particular hurry to be anywhere else.

Dianne heard it before she saw it: the soft roll of wheels on heart pine, the quiet theater of its approach from the kitchen.

It was, as it always was, both of them in miniature. Dianne's sense of tradition and Tamara's sense of spectacle.

Something architectural. Something involving chocolate in a way that required a moment of silence. Something Rafi's grandmother would have recognized and approved of.

Viktor Selin looked at it when it arrived at his table, and he looked at it with the expression of a man who had been in Washington for fourteen months conducting the business of careful nations and had not, until this particular Thursday in this particular room, been given an adequate reason to stay.

He chose something from the cart. He ate it.

He did not look at his watch.

At the bar, Dianne watched him and thought about the week ahead — the confirmation, the President's response, the diplomatic architecture that would need to be built around what Rafi had found, the conversation she would eventually have with the name she had been given, which would be the most sophisticated psychological operation she had ever conducted and which she would conduct in this room, at a round table, in candlelight, with Seymour's music providing the precise acoustic privacy the conversation required.

She thought about the lot behind the building. She thought about what it was waiting to become.

She thought, in the sourceless way she thought the things that lived below the explicable, about a kitchen in New Orleans and a transistor radio and a song that was hers before she knew it was hers.

She looked at her ring.

She looked at her room.

Her golden, engineered, layered, beautiful room — the room she had built from a sketch on a hotel notepad and a lifetime of friendship she could feel but not see, from the lot on the corner and Rafi's four AM financials and Tamara's instinct about the corner booth and Seymour's chord that was also a briefing and twelve steps down from the wainscoting and four hundred meters west to the most powerful office in the world.

She looked at all of it.

She thought: *I built this.* She thought: *I don't know how I knew how.* She thought: *But I did.* She filed it.

Under *pending.* Under the growing, careful, patient file of things she was collecting about herself — the voids and their shapes, the things Tamara almost said, Rafi's eyes, Seymour's certainty about her that had the quality of knowledge rather than assessment — the counter-operation she was running in complete silence on the people who loved her, waiting for the moment when she had enough to present her case.

That moment was coming.

She could feel it the way she felt the songs — not in the mind first but in the body, in the place below the clinical register where the things that were true before she understood them had always lived.

It was coming. She was ready. Not yet.

But soon.

At eleven-forty-five, Viktor Selin folded his napkin in the European manner and rose to leave.

Dianne walked him to the door herself — not a host's gesture exactly, more the gesture of a woman who has decided that a particular guest deserves a particular send-off, which he did, though not for the reasons he understood.

At the door he paused and looked back at the room — the last candles, the dessert cart making its final round, Freeman's guitar resting on its stand while Freeman stood at the edge of the stage talking quietly with Stephon about something that made Stephon laugh, a real laugh, the kind that started in the chest.

"Same time next week?" Selin said. "Same time next week," Dianne said.

He left.

She stood at the door for a moment and watched him go — watched him walk out onto the corner of M and Wisconsin and turn north into the October night with the particular bearing of a man who has decided, without quite knowing when he decided it, that there is somewhere in this city he belongs. She had given him that.

She had given it to him on purpose.

She had given it to him knowing what it would cost him. This was the work.

This was always the work.

She turned back to her room — her golden, still, end-of-evening room, the candles burning low, Seymour covering the piano keys with the care of a man putting something valuable away, Rafi closing his notebook at table four and reaching for the last of his wine.

She walked to table four. She sat across from Rafi. He looked at her.

She looked at him.

"The numbers balanced," she said. "Yes," he said.

"This week?" "This week."

She nodded. She reached across the table and picked up his wine glass and drank what was left of his Meursault and set it back down.

She had no idea why she did it. It felt like something she had always done. It felt older than this room, older than Georgetown, older than the operation and the tunnel and the Thursday they had stood on a sidewalk looking at a corner lot and decided to change their lives. It felt like muscle memory — the body knowing something the mind had not yet been given permission to know.

Rafi watched her do it.

He did not move. He did not look away.

He was running, in the specific and private part of him that the notebooks had been built to hold, a single line of notation: *She reached for my glass.

The way she always reached for my glass when we were twenty and sitting on the porch steps in the evening and the wine was the same wine because neither of us had enough money for two bottles. The way she reached for it then. The same gesture. The same ease. The same absolute absence of self-consciousness.* She does not know she is doing it. She is doing it.

His eyes held what they always held when he looked at her — what she had classified, provisionally, as grief in remission, and what he knew to be something that grief had become across eleven years of patient, daily, private renovation: the specific and earned hope of a man who had never stopped believing in a thing the evidence had sometimes not supported, and who was now, in this room on this Thursday in October, watching the evidence begin to change.

She was beginning to think it might be hope. She was right.

It was hope.

He had been carrying it since the Tuesday the towers fell and he had refused the conclusion the record was reaching. He had been carrying it across the months of the search that produced nothing, through the night at Preservation Hall when knowing replaced believing, through eleven years of notebooks and table four and the footnote on the last page of Volume Fifteen.

He was still carrying it.

He planned to carry it a little further. He was three houses down.

He had always been three houses down. She filed it.

She looked at her room.

She looked at the ring on her hand — the ring that was also a key, that was also a signal, that was also the floor plan of everything they had built together on this corner in this city in this life she had made from materials she could not fully see.

She looked at the door in the far wall that presented itself as wainscoting and behind which twelve steps led down to a round table and a photograph and a tunnel that ran four hundred meters west and at the end of it a door and behind the door a room where the most powerful person in the world sometimes sat in a spare chair and told the truth.

She looked at all of it.

She thought about a kitchen with yellow walls.

She thought about it for a breath. Let it come as close as it came. Did not pursue it. Not yet.

Filed it.

Under *pending.* "Same time next Thursday," she said.

End of Chapter Five

Below the dining room, in the war room twelve steps down, the round table held its photograph in the dark. Two girls on a porch in New Orleans. One pointing.

One laughing.

Outside, the lot behind the restaurant sat cleared and fenced and patient in the October night, the ground holding its question about what it would become, the question addressed to the one person in the world whose answer would determine everything. The amber light in the corridor had returned to green. Seymour locked the bandstand.

Rafi walked home in the dark, his notebook in his inside pocket, seventeen composition notebooks locked in a fireproof safe in his apartment, and one more — the current one, the one he was still filling — ready for whatever Thursday brought next. Tamara sat for a moment alone at the corner booth after everyone had gone.

She ran her hand along the underside of the table until her fingers found the brass plate. She did not need to read it. She knew what it said.

Every truth finds home.

She pressed her palm flat against it for a moment. Then she stood.

She turned off the last light. She left.

The building stood at the corner of M and Wisconsin and held its dark and its history and its secrets and its music still ringing in the plasterwork and its photograph twelve steps below and its tunnel running west and its lot behind waiting and the ring on a woman's hand that was also a key that was also a signal that was also the floor plan of everything they had built together. It had been holding things since 1887. It knew how.

The second novel begins the morning Dianne Montague wakes up and decides it is time to open the file she has been keeping on herself. The lot behind will be ready.

Chapter Six: Who's Keeping Watch

The morning after Thursday was always a Saturday.

This was a fact of the restaurant's week that Dianne had noted early and filed without examination—the way certain facts about a life you are building arrange themselves before you have fully understood what you are building.

Thursday was the operational center. Friday was the decompression, the follow-through, the forensics. Saturday was the morning after the morning after, the hour when the body and the mind, having processed everything they needed to process in the dark, arrived at the kitchen, made coffee, and allowed the week to settle into its final shape.

She was at the restaurant by eight.

She had been at the restaurant by eight every Saturday since they opened, which was a habit she had never consciously decided to form and had never examined closely enough to understand its origin. The truth, if she had stopped to articulate it, was simple: the building was where she thought most clearly, and Saturday morning was the thinking hour. The combination of the two had become the place she came when something needed to be resolved, or when she suspected something had already resolved itself and she merely needed enough quiet to recognize it.

The dining room on Saturday morning was a different room than any other version of itself.

Not the late-night room—all candlelight and music and the warmth of full occupation. Not the four-AM room she had sat in with Jerome and the grid and the analyzer and the baseboard that had been listening since before they opened.

Something quieter than both. The Saturday morning room was the room before it became anything else, when the heart pine floors and the fourteen-foot ceilings and the original plasterwork existed in the specific dignity of a space that knew what it was and did not require anyone present to confirm it. The room did not yet need to perform hospitality. It could simply be itself.

She made coffee in the kitchen and brought it to table four. She sat in Rafi's chair.

She did this sometimes—not deliberately, not as a practice, simply as the thing her body did when the room was empty and the choice of table was hers alone. She had noted it, filed it in the left-hand column of the counter-operation she was running on herself, and not yet annotated it. There were several entries in that column now, each waiting patiently for an explanation she had not yet supplied.

She was sitting in Rafi's chair with her coffee when Antoine arrived at eight-thirty and noted her presence with the particular quality of non-reaction he had developed across the months of working in this building—the recognition that the people in this building arrived and departed and occupied unexpected positions at unexpected hours for reasons that were fully their own and did not require his comment.

"Coffee's fresh," she said.

"Thank you, Chef," he said, which was what Antoine called her when he was being formal, which was what he was always being in the kitchen and never quite being anywhere else, which was one of the many things she liked about him.

She heard him move through the kitchen prep routine—the sounds of a man who had done this enough times to have made it a kind of music, the specific rhythms of mise en place, the knife on the board, the burner clicking to life. The ordinary sounds of a building at work.

She thought about the third chain.

The person in the service position was named Celestine Arceneaux.

She was not Solange Arceneaux's relative, though both women had grown up in the same parish in Louisiana, which was the kind of coincidence that the city of New Orleans produced in sufficient quantity that it had stopped surprising people who were from there. It had not surprised Dianne when Seymour told her. It had confirmed something she had been carrying at the edges of her awareness since the third week of service, when Celestine had appeared in the dining room during a lunch shift and Dianne had experienced, without being able to locate the source of it, the specific sensation of being recognized by someone in a way that did not show on their face.

Celestine Arceneaux was sixty-one years old.

She had been hired as a lunch service attendant—a position that existed in the restaurant's operational structure as a practical necessity and in its intelligence architecture as a gap, a blind spot, the space between the high-operational Thursday evenings and the quiet lunch shifts on which nobody senior was watching the room with their full attention.

A useful position for anyone who preferred not to attract attention.

An even more useful position for someone who understood that attention and observation were not the same thing.

Celestine did not make operational errors.

This was the first thing Seymour had noted about her during the first week of her employment, before the request card, before Jerome's vocal signature match, before any of it—the quality of a person who moved through a room without making the kind of small unnecessary movements that accumulate into a pattern. She served lunch. She spoke when spoken to. She was warm with the guests in the direct, uncomplicated way of a woman from Louisiana who understood that hospitality was not a professional posture but a personal conviction. Guests remembered her without necessarily remembering why, which was often the mark of genuine hospitality rather than performed charm.

She had been in the building every Wednesday lunch service for eleven months. She had been at table twelve last Wednesday.

She had written the request card in block capitals and handed it to Roy Baptiste at the host stand on her way out, which was a casual gesture, the gesture of a regular who had a song she wanted to hear, a gesture so natural that Roy had noted it in the request book under the standard notation without looking up.

She had known he would not look up.

She had timed it for the moment she knew he wouldn't.

Seymour arrived at nine-fifteen.

He came through the kitchen — the route he always used, which was not the front door route, which was not an accident — and found Dianne at table four with her coffee and her legal pad and the expression that meant she had been here for a while and had arrived at something.

He poured his own coffee and sat across from her. "Celestine," she said.

Not a question.

"I ran her," he said. "After I sent you the card. I have been running her since three in the morning."

"And."

"She was born in Vermilion Parish. Moved to New Orleans at seventeen. Worked in the Treme for fifteen years."

He set his cup down. "She worked at a restaurant on Chartres Street. 1987 to 2001."

Dianne looked at him.

Something passed across her face — brief, controlled, the neuropsychologist's trained management of a response that the clinical register wanted to contain and another, older register did not.

"Chartres Street," she said.

"The restaurant three doors down from the house where Dianne Beaumont grew up," Seymour said. The name — her original name, the name before the towers and the wandering and the identity the government had constructed around the woman who arrived in Preservation Hall on a Friday night without knowing where she had come from — landed in the room the way it always landed when Seymour used it. Carefully. With the full acknowledgment of its weight.

Dianne was quiet.

"She knew me," she said. It was not a question either. It was a clinical observation — the forensic psychologist noting a fact and locating it precisely within the architecture of everything else she knew.

"She knew your family," Seymour said. "I believe she has been in this building since before we opened because she was told you were here. Or because she found out you were here and made herself a reason to be near you."

He paused. "The request card is not the first communication. I think it is the most legible one. I think there have been others we haven't recognized as communications because we weren't looking for them."

Dianne looked at the legal pad in front of her.

She had been writing, before Seymour arrived, the things that had arrived in the counter-operation's left-hand column over the past eleven months that she had not been able to source — the small moments of unexplained warmth, the three occasions on which something had been left on her desk that she had not left there, the single Wednesday in March when she had arrived at the restaurant to find a sprig of night-blooming jasmine in a glass on the kitchen pass, which Antoine had seen and not commented on, which she had held for a long time before placing it in a bud vase and setting it on the bar.

Night-blooming jasmine.

The specific plant that grew on the fence of her mother's garden on Chartres Street.

She had known, when she found it, that it meant something. She had not known what it meant.

She knew now.

She looked at Seymour.

"Who told her I was here?" she said.

Seymour met her eyes. "That is the question I have been sitting with since three in the morning," he said. "The answer to that question is either very good news or a different problem entirely."

"It's not a different problem," Dianne said.

She said it with the certainty she used when a clinical assessment was complete — not the certainty of confidence but the certainty of a mind that had arrived at the only conclusion the evidence supported.

"She is not a hostile actor," she said. "The jasmine. Chartres Street. The service position she chose, which put her in the building but never in my direct operational line. The request card — which was addressed to Seymour, not to me, because she understood that the musical intelligence in this room was his domain and she was asking his permission rather than issuing a statement."

She paused. "She is someone who has been watching over me for a long time. Long enough to know what jasmine from Chartres Street meant.

Long enough to know the operational language of a room she researched before she walked into it."

Another pause. "Long enough to know that the song title would reach exactly the two people in this building who would know what it was."

Seymour nodded.

"And Rafi," Dianne said.

"And Rafi," Seymour agreed. "He would have known the song."

"Did he?" "I called him at four in the morning."

The ghost of something crossed Seymour's face — not quite amusement, the emotion adjacent to amusement that exists in people for whom humor and gravity are not opposites but the same weather at different temperatures. "He recognized the title before I finished saying it. He was quiet for about six seconds. Then he said: *She's been there eleven months and neither of us looked.*" Dianne was quiet.

She thought about Rafi at four in the morning — at his desk, at the screens, the seventeenth notebook open, the voice on the phone telling him that a sixty-one year old woman from Vermilion Parish who had worked three doors down from Dianne Beaumont's childhood home on Chartres Street had been serving lunch in this dining room for eleven months without any of them seeing her for what she was.

She thought about what that had cost him. The particular cost of a man who had spent eleven years watching every degree of Dianne's return and had missed this one. Not through inattention. Through the specific blind spot that love creates — the inability to see the things that are hiding in plain sight inside the perimeter of what you are already protecting.

"How is he?" she asked.

Seymour looked at her.

"He's Rafi," he said. "He closed his notebook and said he would be here at nine."

On cue, the kitchen door opened.

Rafi came through with his jacket still on and his notebook in his hand and the look of a man who had been awake since four AM doing the thing he did when the numbers needed to account for something they hadn't accounted for — which was to trace every line of the ledger backward until he found the entry he had missed and understood why he had missed it. He poured coffee.

He sat.

He opened his notebook to a page that had four lines on it.

"Celestine Marie Arceneaux," he said. "Born 1963, Abbeville, Louisiana.

Moved to New Orleans 1980. Employed at Café Beaumont, 1418 Chartres Street, from 1987 until the restaurant closed in September 2001."

He looked up.

"Café Beaumont was owned by Henri Beaumont. Dianne's uncle."

The Saturday morning dining room held this for a moment.

"She worked for my family," Dianne said.

"For fourteen years," Rafi said. "She was the front of house manager when the restaurant closed."

He looked at the notebook. "The restaurant closed three weeks after September 11th. Henri Beaumont closed it because the city was quiet and the foot traffic was gone and because his niece — the woman who had been coming in on Sunday afternoons since she was old enough to sit at a bar stool and order café au lait — was missing."

He closed the notebook.

"She has been looking for you since 2001," he said. "And she found you."

The room was quiet.

Dianne looked at her coffee.

She looked at it with the expression Rafi had been writing entries about in the left-hand pages of seventeen notebooks — the expression of a woman reaching for something that was almost within reach, the specific and recognizable quality of the lacunae shifting, of the material around a gap adjusting to a new pressure.

"An uncle," she said.

"Henri Beaumont," Rafi said. "He's alive. He's eighty-two. He lives in the Lower Ninth Ward in the house he was born in."

He paused. "He has been waiting."

Dianne was very still.

Then she said: "Does he know I'm here?" Rafi looked at her for a moment.

"Celestine found you eight months ago," he said. "She has not told him yet. She wanted to be certain first. That you were—" he stopped. Chose the word carefully. "That you were ready."

The word landed.

Dianne heard it the way she heard everything that lived in the left-hand column — completely, clinically, with the full weight of a woman who had spent thirty years studying the neuroscience of exactly this: the moment when the protection the mind has built around a trauma begins to understand that the trauma is ready to be approached.

Ready.

She had been using that word herself for weeks. Not yet, but soon. Not yet, but the room is almost ready. Not yet, but she is almost ready.

Celestine Arceneaux had been using it for eight months.

They had arrived at the same word from different directions, the way the right word always arrived when it was the true word — from multiple angles simultaneously, until the room had no choice but to fill with it.

"I need to speak to her," Dianne said. "I know," Rafi said.

"Not today."

"I know."

"Thursday," she said.

Rafi looked at her.

"There's a service position open on Thursday evenings," he said. "Roy mentioned it last week. One of the lunch servers asked about picking up Thursday shifts."

"I wonder who," Seymour said.

The ghost of something crossed Dianne's face — not quite the laugh that lived underneath it, the one Rafi had been waiting eleven years to hear again in full, but the movement toward it, the breath before it, the warm anterior to something that was coming. "Put her on the floor Thursday," Dianne said. "The full Thursday operation," Seymour said.

"She's been in this building for eleven months," Dianne said. "She already knows what the operation is. She's been running her own version of it from the lunch shift."

She stood.

She picked up her legal pad.

She looked at the dining room — at its Saturday morning self, spare and honest and entirely itself without ornament.

She thought about a restaurant on Chartres Street three doors down from a house with yellow walls. She thought about a woman who had worked in that restaurant for fourteen years and had spent twenty more looking for the child who used to come in on Sunday afternoons. She thought about a sprig of night-blooming jasmine left on the kitchen pass on a Wednesday in March.

She had known, when she found it, that it meant something. She had been right.

"Saturday morning," she said, to no one in particular, to all of them, to the room. "This is when I think most clearly."

She walked toward the kitchen. At the door she stopped.

She did not turn around. "Rafi," she said.

"Yes," he said.

"The restaurant on Chartres Street. Café Beaumont."

She paused. "Was the food good?" The question arrived in the room with the particular quality of a woman asking about something she could not access and was not asking to access — not yet — but was beginning, carefully, at the edges, to circle. Rafi looked at his coffee.

"It was extraordinary," he said. "Henri Beaumont made the best red beans in the city. Your mother used to say that and then immediately say that her own were better, which made him laugh every single time, and he laughed every single time because he knew she was right and he loved her for saying it anyway."

The kitchen door.

Dianne's hand on the frame. Silence.

"What did I order?" she said. "On Sundays."

Rafi set down his coffee.

He had the entry in the ninth notebook, dated four years ago, which was the last time the Sunday afternoon café au lait had surfaced in what Dianne had said without knowing she was saying it, a fragment rising the way fragments rose — briefly, without context, gone before she could catch it.

He had been waiting for her to ask.

He had been ready to answer for four years.

"Café au lait," he said. "And a beignet. You always ate the beignet before the coffee got cold and then you complained that you'd eaten it too fast. Every Sunday. Since you were seven years old."

The kitchen door.

The Saturday morning room.

The building holding everything it had always held, plus this. Dianne stood at the door for three seconds.

Then she went into the kitchen.

She did not come back for a long time.

Rafi sat at table four and did not open his notebook. Seymour sat across from him and did not speak.

From the kitchen, after a while, came the sound of Antoine explaining something about the Saturday prep — his voice patient, professional, the voice of a man who had made his kitchen a room worth being in — and under it, present, unmistakable, the sound of a woman standing at a prep counter and crying in the specific way of someone who has been given back something they did not know they were missing until the moment it was returned.

Brief.

Controlled.

Real.

Rafi looked at the table.

He looked at the empty coffee cup he had moved to his side of the table without noticing he had moved it. He thought: *there it is.* He thought: *here it comes.* He thought: *she is almost ready.* He thought: *I have been three houses down my whole life and I would not have it any other way and I am ready for the distance to change.* He did not write any of this down.

Some things did not need to be written down.

Some things you simply waited for, in the room you built, on the corner you found, on the Saturday morning when the building held its quiet and the kitchen held its sounds and the woman you had loved since before you had the vocabulary for it stood at a prep counter and cried for the first time in thirty-four years over a café au lait and a beignet. He waited.

In the war room twelve steps below the dining room, the photograph on the round table sat in the light that came through the climate-control vent — the small, steady, amber light of a room that was always in use even when it was empty. Two girls on a porch on Chartres Street. One pointing.

One laughing.

The laughing one had powdered sugar on her chin. Rafi had always loved that detail.

He had written it in the first notebook.

He had written it again in the seventeenth. He would not need to write it again.

Interlude: Celestine

She had found the posting on a Tuesday.

Not the restaurant's posting — there had been no posting, no advertisement, no public announcement of any kind, because Miss Dianne's Jazz and Blues Kitchen did not advertise its staff positions publicly, which was a decision that had been framed in the restaurant's operating philosophy as a commitment to word-of-mouth community hiring and which was, beneath that framing, a security posture.

What she had found was a name.

She had been looking for the name for twenty-two years, which was not the longest she had looked for anything — she had spent thirty looking for her father, and had found him, and the finding had been what findings after long searches always were: more complicated than the looking, more complete than the absence, not what she had expected and exactly what she had needed.

She understood findings.

She understood the difference between the finding and the readiness for the finding.

It was why she had taken the lunch shift and not announced herself.

It was why the jasmine had come first — the smallest legible thing, the thing that would reach only the right person, that would say *I know what this place smells like in summer* without saying anything that required a response.

She had watched, across eleven months of Wednesday lunches and the occasional Thursday she picked up when the floor needed covering, for the signs she knew how to read — the signs she had been reading since the Sunday afternoons when a seven-year-old girl had sat at the bar of her uncle's restaurant on Chartres Street and ordered café au lait with both hands around the cup because the cup was warm and she liked the warmth of it, which was a detail Celestine had written in her own private record not in a notebook but in the way certain memories write themselves into the body and stay there.

She had watched Dianne Montague move through her dining room.

She had watched her stand at the microphone.

She had watched her sit with Rafi at table four on the last Thursday of each month, the way she sat — not across from him but adjacent, turned toward him at the angle of a woman in the company of someone she had known so long that proximity had replaced the need for face-to-face, which was the posture of childhood, of the ease that only early knowing produced. She had watched her reach for his wine glass.

That was the evening she had decided it was time for the request card.

Not because the reaching was the answer — but because the reaching meant the answer was close, and what was close needed a witness who could confirm the direction.

She had written the card in block capitals at the kitchen table in her apartment in Petworth, on a Tuesday night, with a glass of sweet tea and the particular calm of a woman who has carried something for a long time and is finally setting it down somewhere it will be found.

She had chosen the song carefully.

Not a New Orleans song — too legible, too direct, would have told the story before the story was ready to be told. Not a jazz or blues standard — would have been lost in the request book's ordinary volume. A song that was almost unfindable. That lived in the specific and narrow bandwidth between known and forgotten where messages hide that are meant for the people who know where to listen.

Seymour Emerson would know. She had done her research.

Seymour Emerson knew everything that had ever been recorded.

And the title — the specific plain language of a working man's Southern rock song from a session that had never reached beyond a four-county radius in Alabama in 1974 — said exactly what she needed to say.

Who's keeping watch of my old lady.

Not surveillance. Not threat. A question from someone who had been keeping watch for twenty-two years and was asking the room whether it understood what it was holding, whether the people in it knew what they had, whether they were watching carefully enough to protect what was about to become available.

She had handed the card to Roy Baptiste on her way out. She had not looked back.

She had gone home and eaten her dinner and gone to bed and slept the sleep of a woman who has done the thing she came to do and is prepared to wait for the answer in the language the room chose to send it.

The answer had come the following Thursday.

Three notes, embedded in the opening bars of *Autumn Leaves.* Transposed. Brief. Unremarkable to anyone not listening for them. She had been listening.

She had set down her tray in the service corridor and stood very still and let the three notes land.

They said: *we hear you. We know what you are. You are not alone in this.* She had picked up her tray.

She had gone back to work.

She had cried in the walk-in cooler between the salad course and the entrée, briefly and completely, with the door closed, in the way of a woman who has been carrying something for twenty-two years and has just been told by a man at a piano that she does not have to carry it alone anymore. She had washed her face at the prep sink.

She had gone back to the floor.

She was, in all the ways that mattered, ready for Thursday.

Two floors below the dining room, in the corridor that ran west beneath Georgetown Drive Drive, the amber light held steady. The tunnel did not know about Celestine Arceneaux.

The tunnel only knew what moved through it.

But the building above it — the Federal-period brick building on the corner of M Street and Wisconsin, the building that had been holding things since 1887 — knew. It had been holding her too.

Since the first Wednesday she walked through the service entrance with her references and her résumé and her careful, unremarkable face and her twenty- two years of looking, and looked up at the fourteen-foot ceilings and the heart pine floors and the round tables and knew, without anyone telling her, that she was in the right room. She had always known how to find the right room.

She had learned it from a woman who ordered café au lait with both hands around the cup. The building held this too. It knew how.

Chapter Seven: Celestine's Thursday

She arrived at five-fifteen.

This was thirty minutes before the floor staff call time, which Roy Baptiste had given her as five forty-five when he put her on the Thursday roster, and which she had noted and disregarded, because Celestine Arceneaux had spent twenty-two years in fine dining service and understood that the first time you work a new floor you arrive early enough to read the room before the room begins to read you.

She came through the service entrance.

The kitchen was already alive — Antoine at the center of it with the focused authority of a man for whom the Thursday dinner rush was not a challenge but a recitation, the prep line moving in the practiced rhythms of a crew that had found its stride. She nodded to Antoine. He nodded back. She had worked his lunch kitchen for eleven months and they had developed the specific and sufficient understanding of two people who respected each other's competence and did not require conversation to confirm it. She hung her coat.

She found the linen station. She began to fold napkins.

This was not in her Thursday instructions. Roy had told her she was on the floor, not at the linen station. But her hands needed something to do while her eyes did their work, and her eyes were doing their work — reading the room before service, cataloguing the table configuration, noting the placement of the round tables and the specific geometry of the bandstand and the relationship between the service corridor and the dining room floor that she had spent eleven months studying from the lunch shift perspective and was now seeing, for the first time, in the full Thursday dress.

The room was different at Thursday scale.

Not larger — the square footage was the same, the ceilings the same fourteen feet, the heart pine floors the same warm continuity. Different in the way that a room is different when it is fully itself rather than partially itself.

The candles were being lit. The flowers on the round tables — white and cream, Tamara's standing order, the aesthetic she had argued for in the third week of renovation and which Dianne had approved without asking why, because Tamara's eye for a room was the kind of eye you trusted without the footnotes — were fresh from that morning's delivery. The lighting was transitioning from afternoon to evening, the dimmers moving through the sequence that Tamara had designed and that Dianne had memorized and that the room's regulars recognized as the signal that the evening was becoming what it became.

Celestine folded napkins and read the room and was ready.

She saw Dianne at seven forty-five.

Dianne came down the back stairs in ivory silk — the Thursday silk, the Thursday descent, the particular quality of a woman who had understood since she first walked into a room that the way you arrived was information and that information given freely was information wasted. She came down the stairs at the pace of someone who owned the floor she was about to reach and knew it but did not need to announce it, which was the pace Celestine remembered from the Sunday afternoons on Chartres Street — when a seven-year-old girl in a school dress had come through the door of Café Beaumont with her mother and walked directly to the bar stool and climbed up without hesitation, the movement of a child who knew where she was going because she had been there enough times to own it — and Celestine, who had been twenty-four and had only been at the restaurant for two months, had looked at the child and thought: that one has decided how she is going to take up space in the world. She had been right.

Dianne reached the bottom of the stairs.

She crossed the dining room with the ease of a woman walking through her own home — touching the back of a chair in passing, exchanging a word with Roy at the host stand, reading the reservation book with the particular speed of a mind processing names as information rather than inventory. She did not look at the linen station.

She was not supposed to look at the linen station. Thursday was a performance in the fullest sense, and a performance required the performer to inhabit the role completely — the proprietor of the finest intimate jazz room in Georgetown and nothing else, nothing that acknowledged the layers.

She did not look at the linen station.

But she paused — one half-step, almost invisible, the pause of a person whose peripheral field has registered something and whose body has responded before the mind has given permission — and then continued.

Celestine had been watching for that pause. She had found it.

She went back to her napkins.

Seymour arrived at the bandstand at eight-fifteen.

Celestine was at the service bar when he came through — she heard him before she saw him, the particular footfall of someone who moved through this space as though the floor knew him, which it did. She watched him cross to the piano from the corner of her eye.

She watched him sit.

She watched him adjust the bench — the precise, private ritual of a pianist finding his relationship with the instrument before he began — and place his hands on the keys without playing. He looked across the room.

He found her at the service bar.

Their eyes met for exactly one second. He gave no sign.

She gave no sign.

Then his hands found the opening chord of *Autumn Leaves* and the room exhaled and became what it always became when Seymour began — the dining room, the Thursday room, the room that had been waiting all week to be this.

In the opening bars, between the third and the fourth measure, in a place where the voicing shifted into something slightly different — a touch, a color, a choice of note so small that no one in the room would register it as a choice at all — three notes.

Transposed. Brief. Present.

The question she had asked him. And his answer: *We hear you. We know what you are. Welcome to Thursday.* Celestine set down the bread basket at table fourteen and said something pleasant to the couple seated there and straightened and looked at the bandstand for one second.

She nodded once.

Then she went back to work.

9:01 PM Dianne sang the first song at nine o'clock. I'd Rather Go Blind.

Celestine was clearing the entrée course from table sixteen when the first notes landed — Seymour's piano, the opening figure, the specific unhurried patience of a song that understands it does not need to rush because what it has to say will be heard — and she stopped.

Just for a moment.

The kind of stopping the body does when it receives something the mind is not yet ready to process — the brief involuntary stillness of a person being taken somewhere they did not fully choose to go.

She had heard recordings of Etta James's version. She had heard other singers cover it. She had not heard it like this — the voice coming from a woman standing at a microphone in a room in Georgetown that contained, among other things, the most consequential missing piece of the last twenty-two years of her life.

Freeman's harmony arrived beneath Dianne's lead the way it always arrived — not intruding but completing, the third below that made the melody suddenly whole, that transformed a voice into a conversation. Dixie's alto came in under both of them. Tamara filled the spaces that only Tamara filled. Four voices.

Celestine set down the cleared plates at the service station and stood for a moment with her hands at her sides and let the song reach her.

She had spent twenty-two years looking. She was here now.

The woman she had been looking for was on that stage. She was singing.

The room was full and warm and golden and the song was moving through it the way songs moved through Miss Dianne's — not as performance but as weather, not as entertainment but as truth — and Celestine Arceneaux, sixty-one years old, from Vermilion Parish, Louisiana, standing at the service station with a cleared entrée course and twenty-two years behind her, felt something she had not felt since the Tuesday in September when the city went quiet and the search began and the search did not end.

She felt: *here.* Not *there.* Not *almost.* Not *waiting.* Here.

She picked up her tray.

She went back to the floor.

She worked the second course. She worked the dessert service. She cleared and reset and smiled at her tables and fetched the wine and answered the questions guests asked about the menu in the warm and direct manner she had been deploying in dining rooms for twenty-two years.

She did her job.

Because that was what you did in a room like this.

You did your job until the job gave you the moment it was holding.

11:47 PM The last guests were finding their coats.

The dessert cart had made its final round. Freeman's guitar was on its stand. Seymour's hands rested on the piano keys in the posture of a man whose evening had been complete.

Roy Baptiste was walking the last guests to the door with the graceful theater of a floor manager who understood that the farewell was as important as the greeting.

Celestine was resetting table seventeen. She heard footsteps on the floor behind her. She did not turn.

She knew the footstep. Had learned it across eleven months of Wednesdays — the specific and unhurried pace of a woman who moved through her own building with the full and unperformed authority of someone who had decided on arrival and had not revised the decision since.

Dianne stopped behind her. Celestine set the last fork. Straightened the napkin.

Turned around.

They looked at each other.

The last candle on the table between them was burning low — an hour of light left in it at most, the flame steady in the still air of the post-service room.

Celestine was sixty-one and had the face of a woman who had done a great deal of outdoor living and had decided some years ago that the sun had earned the right to show on her and she had earned the right to let it. Her hair was silver and close-cropped and her eyes were the specific dark brown of someone from the Louisiana delta country who had the particular ability to look at a person and mean it, without performance, without softening. She was looking at Dianne.

She was meaning it.

Dianne looked back.

The clinical register was running — she could not turn it off, did not want to turn it off. Age. History. The specific way long-held emotion organized itself in the musculature around the eyes. The involuntary tension at the jaw that meant someone was managing something real and succeeding at it and had been succeeding for a long time.

But beneath the clinical register, something else was running. Something older and less organized and less willing to be managed.

The body's knowledge. The specific recognition that preceded the mind's confirmation. The feeling of a room she had been in and could not remember being in — the warmth of it, the smell of it, the specific combination of café au lait and frying beignets and something else, something green and night-blooming that lived at the edges of every summer memory she had ever almost caught.

She knew this face.

She did not know how she knew it. She knew it.

“I remember you,” she said.

She said it quietly. Without theater. The way you say something you have not planned to say and find, in the saying of it, that it is true.

Celestine’s jaw moved once — the controlled movement of a woman pressing something down, successfully, with long practice. Her eyes did not change.

They had held this moment in their expectation for twenty-two years and they were not going to break it now.

“You used to ask for extra powdered sugar,” Celestine said. “Your uncle always said you’d had enough and then he’d put more on when your mother wasn’t looking.”

A breath.

The candle.

The last guests’ voices at the door, fading. “Henri,” Dianne said.

Not a question. The name arriving the way names arrived in the counter-operation’s left-hand column — not remembered but recognized, the difference between recovering something lost and finding something that had been present all along at the edge of the available.

“He’s in the Lower Ninth,” Celestine said. “The house on Delery Street. The one he was born in.”

She paused. “He planted jasmine on the south fence fifteen years ago. He said your mother told him once that jasmine was the smell of a woman who knew what she wanted.”

The dining room.

The candle.

Dianne's hands at her sides — still, the specific stillness of a woman who was not suppressing but receiving, letting the information arrive in its own order without forcing it into a sequence she could control.

"Is he well?" she said.

"He is eighty-two and stubborn," Celestine said. "He planted a garden in his seventies. He makes red beans every Monday. He has a radio in the kitchen that he has not moved in forty years and he plays it at the same volume he played it when you sat at his bar and ordered café au lait with both hands around the cup."

Dianne looked at the table between them. At the napkin she had just straightened.

"He would want to see you," Celestine said. "When you're ready. There is no urgency. He has waited twenty-two years."

She paused. "He would say that a woman who takes care of her own readiness is a woman worth waiting for."

"Did he say that?" "He says it every time I call him," Celestine said. "Which is every Sunday."

Dianne looked at her.

For a long time. With the full weight of her attention — the clinical register, the body's knowledge, the thirty years of professional practice and the seven years of Sunday afternoons on Chartres Street that lived somewhere below the professional practice, the years she could not open and could feel through the wall like heat through brick.

"Who told you I was here?" she said. Celestine held her gaze.

"I found your name on a restaurant filing three years ago," she said. "In the District's business registration records. Dianne Montague, registered agent for a limited liability company acquiring a property at M and Wisconsin."

A pause. “The name was different. But I knew the handwriting.”

Dianne looked at her.

“The filing was handwritten,” Celestine said. “The attorney’s office was supposed to type it. But the signature line — the beneficial owner’s signature — was in a hand I had been looking at since 1987. On the order tickets at my uncle’s restaurant. On the birthday cards he kept in the drawer behind the bar.”

She stopped. “You always made your lowercase a the same way.

Open at the top. Like a letter that isn’t finished. I used to think your penmanship teacher must have despaired.”

The lowest laugh in the world.

It was not loud. It was not long. It arrived in Dianne’s throat and left before she fully chose it — the laugh of a woman in whom something was moving that had been still for a very long time. Not the full laugh, not yet, but the leading edge of it, the sound of something approaching that had been approaching slowly and was now close enough to hear.

Celestine heard it.

She pressed her jaw once.

“I will be here every Thursday,” Celestine said. “And every Wednesday lunch. I will be here until you don’t need me here, or until you tell me you don’t, or until Henri runs out of patience, which will not be soon because Henri Beaumont has the patience of a man who was born in New Orleans and has survived everything New Orleans has asked him to survive and has decided that patience is not a virtue but a discipline.”

She picked up her tray.

She looked at Dianne one more time.

"He keeps your photograph on the kitchen table," she said. "The one with you and the other girl on the porch. He found it in a box of your mother's things after Katrina. He has kept it on the kitchen table since 2005."

She went back to work.

Dianne stood at table seventeen with the candle burning beside her and her hands at her sides and the room settling into its end-of-service quiet around her and let all of it arrive — not pursuing, not managing, not applying the clinical register to the temperature of the material.

Just receiving it.

The way the room received the music.

Completely. Without judgment. With the full attentiveness of a space that had been built for exactly this.

Rafi was at the bar when she found him.

He was sitting on one of the bar stools at the far end — not at table four, not with his notebook, but on a bar stool with his jacket over the stool beside him and his glass of Meursault in his hand, which was where he sat on the evenings after a full operational Thursday when he needed the informality of the bar rather than the structure of the table.

She sat on the stool beside his jacket.

He moved the jacket to his lap without comment.

She picked up his wine glass and drank what remained and set it back down. He signaled for the bottle.

Roy, who was breaking down the host stand and who had the particular quality of selective attention that every great floor manager develops — seeing everything, responding to what required response, leaving the rest exactly where it was — poured without approaching.

Dianne looked at the bar.

She looked at the bottles in their rows — the amber and the gold and the deep dark of the spirits she had chosen for this room with Tamara and Rafi across three weeks of tastings in the private dining room two years ago, each bottle a considered decision, each placement deliberate.

"An open lowercase a," she said. Rafi looked at her.

"She recognized my handwriting on the business filing," Dianne said. "The signature on the beneficial owner line. She knew the way I make a lowercase a."

She paused. "She has known it since 1987."

Rafi was quiet for a moment.

"You always wrote it that way," he said. "Open at the top. Your third-grade teacher wrote a note to your mother about it. She said it looked like the letter was asking a question."

He paused. "Your mother kept the note."

Dianne turned the wine glass in her hands.

"There is a photograph on Henri Beaumont's kitchen table," she said. "He found it in a box of my mother's things after Katrina. The one with me and the other girl on the porch."

Rafi was very still.

"He has kept it on the kitchen table since 2005."

"Yes."

She looked at him.

He looked back.

The bar between them. The bottles in their rows. The last candle somewhere in the dining room burning toward its end. The building breathing around them in the way it breathed at the end of a long Thursday — slowly, fully, with the particular satisfaction of a structure that had done what it was built to do.

"He has two photographs," Rafi said, after a moment. "He has the one from the porch, which was your mother's. And he has one from a Sunday in 1991 when your mother brought a camera to the restaurant and took photographs of everyone. Henri at the bar. Your mother at the corner table. Celestine in the service corridor."

He paused. "And you. On the bar stool. With your café au lait. Both hands around the cup."

Dianne looked at the window. At the October dark beyond it.

"I want to go to New Orleans," she said. Rafi looked at her.

Not with surprise. The expression of a man who had been waiting for a sentence and had been certain of its arrival and was experiencing, now that it had arrived, the specific and irreplaceable feeling of a thing you have been holding toward reaching its destination.

"When?" he said.

"Not yet," she said. "But soon."

She turned the wine glass.

"I need to open the file first," she said. Rafi was very still.

"The file you've been keeping on yourself," he said. "Yes."

A long moment.

"I know about the file," he said.

"I know you know," she said. Another moment.

"I can help," he said. "When you're ready."

She looked at him.

The bar light caught the ring on her right hand — the dark metal alloy, the eight-millimeter width, the matte finish containing on its inner surface the floor plan of everything they had built together, everything that was above them and below them and around them and running west beneath the avenue and branching, they now understood, in more directions than they had mapped.

"I know," she said.

She set down the glass.

She slid off the bar stool.

She stood for a moment with her hand on the bar — not holding it, just present, the light touch of a woman locating herself before she moved.

"The file is in my office," she said. "The third floor. The room that isn't on the floor plan."

"I know where it is," Rafi said.

"I know you do."

She looked at him. "Monday morning. I'll be here at seven."

"I'll bring coffee," he said.

She nodded.

She walked toward the kitchen — the stairs, the third floor, the room that didn't exist on any document — and Rafi sat at the bar with the Meursault and the jacket in his lap and the building breathing around him and the wine glass she had been holding still warm in his hand where he'd picked it up after she set it down.

He turned it slowly. He looked at the bar.

He thought: *Monday.* He thought: *here it comes.* He thought: *I have been three houses down my whole life.* He thought: *the distance is about to change.* He set down the glass.

He picked up the seventeenth notebook and opened it to the left-hand page and wrote in the small private handwriting: Thursday. She said: I want to go to New Orleans. She said: I need to open the file first.

She said: Monday morning.

He looked at what he had written.

He added: *Seventeen years. Not yet. But here.* He closed the notebook.

He put on his jacket.

He walked out into the October night and turned north on Wisconsin and walked home in the dark, and the building stood at the corner behind him and held its light and its photographs and its baseboard and its tunnel and its lot behind waiting and its third floor room that wasn't on any floor plan, and the amber light in the corridor ran steady.

The building knew what was coming.

Not by prediction but by the accumulated weight of everything it had been asked to hold, which was considerable, and which it had held without complaint since 1887.

It knew how.

End of Chapter Seven

Tamara was the last to leave, as she was always the last to leave.

She sat for a moment in the corner booth — the seat that had been built to feel held rather than trapped, the blue-black leather, the brass plate on the underside of the table — and she put her hand flat against the plate and held it there. She had heard the laugh.

It had come from the direction of table seventeen and it had been brief and unguarded and small, the laugh of a woman who had not chosen to laugh and had laughed anyway, and Tamara had been at the service bar when it happened and she had set down the glass she was holding and stood very still and let it reach her. She had been waiting for that laugh for twenty-two years.

Longer, if you counted the before — and she always counted the before, because the before was hers to count, because she was the one who carried it. She pressed her palm flat against the plate. Every truth finds home.

She had believed this when she chose the words. She believed it more now.

She sat in the corner booth for a long time after the building had gone quiet, and the candle on the table nearest her burned all the way down, and the wax pooled and hardened, and the room held its dark and its warmth and the residue of the music still alive in the plasterwork, and the memory of a laugh that had lasted half a second and changed the shape of everything. Then she stood.

She turned off the last light. She left.

Chapter Eight: The File

Monday morning.

She was at the restaurant at six-fifty, which was ten minutes before she had told Rafi she would be there and which she had known she would be. The building at six-fifty on a Monday in late October was the building at its most itself — the week not yet started, the service days ahead still future, the particular quality of a structure in its own company that old buildings have and new ones do not.

She made coffee.

She took it up the back stairs to the third floor.

She went through the wall panel in the private dining room — the door that presented itself as wainscoting, that required the ring's proximity to open, that she had passed through three hundred times and that today she passed through with the specific awareness of a woman who understood she was crossing a threshold that was not only architectural.

The third floor office was small and book-lined and contained a desk and two chairs and a window that looked onto a light well and received three hours of direct sun in the late morning. The sun came through the light well and hit the wall of books and made the room look like something that had been here for centuries, which in its bones it had been.

The file was in the bottom drawer of the desk.

She had put it there fourteen months ago, when she had understood that she was building a counter-operation and that the counter-operation required a physical record, because the most important evidence always existed in physical form.

She had built the file from the left-hand pages of her own notebooks — not the operational notebooks, which lived in the war room and the office safe, but the smaller ones, the ones with the dark green cover that she had been buying at the same stationer's on Georgetown Drive Drive since they opened.

The green notebooks were not classified. They were not addressed to anyone.

They were the record of the things she noticed without knowing why she noticed them — the inventory of the voids and their shapes, the catalog of what Tamara almost said and what Rafi's eyes held and what Seymour's certainty felt like from the inside of being certain about, and the specific and recurring quality of certain smells and sounds and textures that arrived without origin and carried without context the weight of something she had known and had been removed from the knowing of.

She had seventeen green notebooks.

The same number as Rafi's composition books.

She had never counted his. She knew the number because she had noted it in the fourteenth green notebook, on a Thursday evening when she was sitting at table four after service and Rafi had been at the bar and she had looked at his inside jacket pocket and thought, with the clarity of a clinical observation: *he is on his seventeenth,* and had not known how she knew.

She had written: *I know he is on his seventeenth. I don't know how I know. Filed under: things the body knows before the mind has been given permission.* She opened the file.

The file was organized the way she organized everything — from the foundational outward, from the established to the emerging. The earliest material at the bottom, the most recent at the top. A structure that required you to work backward to understand it, which was intentional, which was the architecture of a mind that understood that the truth of a person was almost always found at the origin rather than the surface.

She began at the top.

She read for forty minutes before Rafi knocked.

Three taps. The knock he used for her specifically — unhurried, the knock of a man who was not uncertain about his welcome but who understood that welcome was not the same as readiness and that the distinction deserved acknowledgment.

"Come in," she said.

He came in with two coffees and closed the door and sat in the second chair across from her desk. He handed her the coffee. He looked at the window — the light well, the October sky above it, grey this morning, the particular grey of a city that had decided winter was coming and was not going to pretend otherwise.

He did not look at the file. She appreciated this.

"There is a question," Dianne said, "that is at the bottom of the file."

"I know," he said.

"It is the question the file was built to answer."

"I know."

She looked at him.

"I need you to tell me what you know," she said. "Not what you think I can hear. Not what you've decided is the right sequence. What you know."

Rafi looked at the window for a moment. He looked at his coffee.

He looked at her.

"You were in New York on the morning of September eleventh, 2001," he said. The office.

The grey light.

The file on the desk between them.

"You had been in New York for three days," he said. "A conference. The conference was at the World Trade Center. You were in the North Tower at eight forty-six in the morning."

Dianne was very still.

"You got out," he said. "The records — the official records, the records that said what happened to the people in the building — don't have you getting out. Because you didn't go to the hospital. Because you didn't go to a shelter.

Because the person who walked out of the building at eight forty-seven that morning walked out without —" He stopped. Chose the next word with the care he brought to every word that mattered. "Without the architecture of herself intact."

The clinical vocabulary arrived and Dianne let it arrive — dissociative amnestic episode, hippocampal disruption, the failure of memory consolidation under extreme trauma, the specific and sometimes permanent severance between episodic memory and the continuous narrative of self. She had written three academic papers on this. She had not written about herself in any of them.

She had always known, in the part of her mind that the lacunae had not reached, what the lacunae were protecting her from knowing.

She had simply not been ready to know it yet. She was ready now.

"The wandering," she said.

"Five months," Rafi said. "Between September and February. We don't know the full geography of it. Seymour has pieces. I have pieces."

He paused. "You ended up in New Orleans because you were from New Orleans. The body knows the direction home even when the mind has lost the address."

She thought about Preservation Hall.

She thought about a Friday night in February and a man at a piano whose music she had recognized before she had recognized the man.

"Seymour found me," she said.

"Seymour was looking," Rafi said. "He had been looking since October. He went to New York in October and found the last trace of you — a shelter intake record from the night of the eleventh, signed with your middle name, which you had done instinctively, the clinical version of hiding while not hiding."

He paused. "He tracked the middle name forward and lost it in November and picked it up again in New Orleans in January. He was in Preservation Hall that Friday because he had reason to believe you were there."

"And you," she said.

Rafi was quiet for a moment.

"I drove to Frenchmen Street in eleven minutes," he said. "Which was four minutes faster than the route permitted."

She looked at him.

He looked at her.

"Three houses down," she said.

It was the first time she had said it. Not as a question — she had known it for weeks, had let it arrive and had not pursued it and had been letting it become more available every day, the way the things in the left-hand column became available when the counter-operation had built enough of the surrounding structure to hold them.

"Three houses down," he said. She looked at the file.

She looked at the seventeen green notebooks.

She thought about a kitchen with yellow walls, which she had been thinking about for weeks with increasing frequency and increasing tolerance for the thinking — letting herself stay in the image longer each time, the way you rebuild tolerance for a sensation by incremental exposure, which was the oldest and most reliable clinical method and which she had been applying to herself with the same rigor she would apply to a patient and with the additional complication of being both the clinician and the subject.

Yellow walls.

A transistor radio.

A song that was hers before she knew it was hers.

"What song was playing in the kitchen," she said. "What did she play on the radio."

Rafi looked at her for a long moment.

"It changed," he said. "On Mondays she played the jazz station. On Saturdays she played the blues. On Sunday mornings she played whatever the gospel station had."

He paused. "But on Thursday evenings — when she was cooking dinner and you were at the kitchen table doing your homework and the screen door was open and the jasmine was coming through from the garden — on Thursday evenings she played whatever she felt like. Which was usually Etta James. Or Dinah Washington. Or occasionally Nina Simone when she was in a particular mood."

Dianne looked at the window.

At the grey October sky above the light well. I'd Rather Go Blind.

What A Difference A Day Makes. Feeling Good.

The songs she had chosen for Thursday evenings in this room, assembled over two years with Seymour, selected by the instinct of a woman who understood music as excavation without knowing what she was excavating toward.

The songs her mother had played on Thursday evenings in a kitchen with yellow walls.

She did not cry.

She was past the crying — that had happened in Antoine's kitchen on Saturday morning and it had been brief and complete and had done what it needed to do, the way good crying always did: cleared something, opened something, created the space for the next thing to arrive.

What arrived now was not grief but recognition.

The specific, irreversible, full-body recognition of a person arriving at a truth they have been approaching for a long time and have now reached.

She looked at Rafi.

He was looking at her with the expression she had spent eleven months classifying and reclassifying — grief in remission, then hope, then the specific and earned hope of a man who had been carrying something for twenty-two years and was watching it be received.

"She would have been proud of this room," Dianne said.

"She would have claimed she taught you everything you know," Rafi said. "And she would have been right and known she was right and been too proud to say so directly. She would have sat at table four — your table, because she would have found the table that was yours within ten minutes of arriving — and she would have ordered the red beans and rice and she would have told Antoine that Henri's were better and she would have laughed when Antoine disagreed, and she would have been in that chair every Thursday until the building turned her away, which it never would have."

Dianne looked at the file.

At the seventeen green notebooks.

At the bottom of the file, which she had not yet reached, but which she could feel the weight of — the foundational material, the earliest entries, the question the file had been built to answer.

She thought about Henri Beaumont in the house on Delery Street with the photograph on the kitchen table and the jasmine on the south fence and the red beans on Mondays and the forty-year-old radio.

She thought about a woman who ordered café au lait with both hands around the cup because the cup was warm and she liked the warmth of it.

"I need to call him," she said. Rafi looked at her.

"Henri," she said. "I'm not ready to go yet. But I need to call him."

"I know his number," Rafi said.

"I know you do."

He took out his phone.

He set it on the desk between the file and the coffee cups. He looked at her.

She looked at the phone. She picked it up.

She dialed.

It rang four times — the four rings of a man who was not young and was not in a hurry and believed that a telephone ringing deserved to be answered when you were ready and not before.

On the fourth ring: a voice.

Deep. Unhurried. The voice of a man from New Orleans who had been born in a house in the Lower Ninth Ward and had lived in it through everything the city had asked him to live through and had not left and would not leave.

“Hello,” the voice said.

Dianne looked at the grey light above the light well. She thought about a bar stool.

She thought about both hands around a cup. She thought about powdered sugar.

“Uncle Henri,” she said.

Across the line, a silence. Two seconds.

Two seconds was a long time.

Two seconds was twenty-two years condensed to the width of a breath.

Then the voice said — not breaking, not performing, not reaching for the register of emotion the moment deserved because the moment was already too large for reaching toward it and the only way through it was to be still and speak plainly, which was a thing Henri Beaumont had always known how to do, which was a thing she was only now remembering that she had always loved about him — “I knew you’d call on a Monday,” he said. Dianne was quiet for a moment.

“How did you know Monday?” she said.

“Because your mother always sorted her hardest things on Monday mornings,” he said. “She said it was the best day for it. The week ahead of you, the week behind you, nothing in between except what needed doing."

A pause. "You were always your mother's child."

The office.

The grey light.

Rafi very still in the second chair, his hands around his coffee, looking at the window.

The file on the desk.

Seventeen green notebooks in a column.

Dianne turned the phone in her hand and looked at the light well and thought about a Monday morning in a kitchen with yellow walls and a woman sorting the hardest things with the week spread out on both sides of her like something navigable, like something that could be crossed if it was approached one task at a time, one meal at a time, one day at a time.

"I'm in Washington," she said. "I have a restaurant."

"I know," Henri said. "Celestine told me about the restaurant. She said the music is extraordinary."

"It is," Dianne said. "I sing on Thursdays."

A sound from across the line—not a laugh exactly, something older than a laugh, the sound of a man receiving confirmation of something he had believed without evidence for a long time, as though a piece of a pattern he had carried privately for years had just settled into place.

"Of course you do," he said. "Your mother sang on Thursdays too. In the kitchen. While she cooked."

The line held them both for a moment. The October morning.

The light well.

Four hundred miles south, in a house on Delery Street, an eighty-two-year-old man standing at the kitchen counter with a telephone and a photograph on the table behind him and the jasmine coming in through the south window even in October because he tended it and it rewarded the tending.

For a moment Dianne could see the room without having ever entered it. The stove. The counter. The photograph. The familiar order of a life maintained with care. She could picture Henri standing there as easily as she could picture her mother in the yellow kitchen years ago, and the realization carried with it a strange and unexpected comfort.

"I'm not ready to come yet," Dianne said. "I need a little more time."

"Take what you need," Henri said. "The house isn't going anywhere. I'm not going anywhere." Another pause. "I have red beans on the stove right now. I'll put some in the freezer for when you come."

The lowest and most private laugh in the world arrived for the second time in four days—brief, unguarded, the sound of a woman in whom something enormous was moving toward its resolution.

Not finished.

Not resolved.

But moving.

The way ice moves on a river at the beginning of spring—slowly at first, almost imperceptibly, until suddenly the whole current is in motion and it becomes impossible to remember a time when it seemed still.

"Save me the cornbread too," she said.

"I always make too much," he said. "I always have."

She looked at Rafi.

He was looking at his coffee with the expression of a man in the presence of something he has been holding toward for twenty-two years and is now watching arrive and is managing, with his full capability, the fullness of it.

He was not entirely succeeding. She looked at the window.

"Henri," she said. "The photograph on your kitchen table. The one with me and the other girl on the porch."

"Yes," he said.

"Her name is Tamara," Dianne said. "She's here. In Washington. She's been here the whole time."

Across the line, the particular quality of a silence that was not absence but receipt — a man absorbing information that completed something he had been carrying incompletely for a long time.

"Is she well?" he said.

"She is," Dianne said. "She runs the front of house. She chose the flowers and the corner booth and the brass plate under the table that says: *every truth finds home.*" "That sounds right," Henri said softly. "That sounds exactly right."

The Monday morning.

The light well brightening as the sun found its angle.

The file on the desk not yet finished but no longer the heaviest thing in the room.

"I'll call you Sunday," Dianne said.

"I'll be here," he said. "I'm always here on Sundays."

“I know,” she said. And then, because it was true and because the truth had been available to her for three days and she had been letting it arrive at its own pace and it had arrived: “I remember Sundays.”

The line was quiet for a moment.

When Henri spoke again his voice was the same—deep, unhurried, the voice of a man who had decided decades ago that steadiness was the highest form of love and had practiced it accordingly—but beneath it something had shifted, the almost imperceptible redistribution of a weight, the sound of a man who had been standing in one posture for twenty-two years and had just been given permission to stand differently.

"The café au lait is better now," he said. "I learned a new method. Your mother would have argued with me about it.”

"She would have said hers was better," Dianne said. "She would have been right," he said.

She smiled.

The office seemed to hold the moment—the smile, the grey light turning gold as the sun moved across the light well, the building breathing quietly around her, the file on the desk, the notebooks, the ring on her hand, the second chair where Rafi sat very still with his hands around his coffee, not looking directly at her because he understood that some moments required privacy even in company, which was one of the thousand things she had always known about him without ever quite knowing how she knew.

"Sunday," she said. "Sunday," he said. She ended the call.

She set the phone on the desk. She looked at Rafi.

He looked at her.

"She made café au lait on Thursday evenings," Dianne said. "My mother. In the kitchen. While the radio played.”

"Yes," Rafi said.

"And I did my homework at the kitchen table."

"You always finished it before dinner," he said. "Even when you didn't want to. She had a rule about it."

"The screen door," Dianne said.

"Was always open in the summer," he said. "Until September."

For a moment neither of them said anything.

The memory sat comfortably between them, not needing explanation. It belonged to a world so complete in its particulars that a screen door was enough to summon the whole of it—the kitchen, the radio, the smell of coffee and dinner, the long summer evenings before either of them understood how much of a life could be shaped by ordinary rituals, or how fiercely those rituals would be remembered once they were gone.

Then she looked at the file.

She looked at the bottom of it—the foundational material, the earliest entries, the question that the file had been built to answer, which she now understood was not a single question but a corridor of questions, each opening onto the next, each requiring the one before it to be answered first. The deeper she went, the more she understood that the file had never been an investigation into a single event. It was a reconstruction, a patient assembling of causes and consequences, losses and survivals, all of them leading toward something larger than the people who had first created it.

And she had answered the first one that morning on the telephone with a man standing in a kitchen four hundred miles south, with red beans on the stove and a photograph on the table and twenty-two years of Sundays behind him. She had answered it not by discovering something new, but by recognizing something that had been waiting for recognition all along.

She had answered the first one.

There were others.

"I need to read to the bottom," she said. "I know," Rafi said.

"It will take time."

"I know."

"Will you stay?" He looked at her.

He looked at her with the full weight of seventeen composition notebooks and twenty-two years and the drive to Frenchmen Street in eleven minutes and the footnote on the last page of Volume Fifteen and the lot behind the building, cleared and fenced and patient.

And he said the only thing there was to say, which was also the truest thing, the thing he had been ready to say since the Tuesday the towers fell and he had refused the record's conclusion: "I have been staying," he said. "Since before you knew I was here."

The gold light continued its slow movement through the light well.

The building held its Monday morning quiet. The file lay open on the desk.

Waiting.

Not urgently.

Patiently.

The way certain truths wait when they know they will eventually be reached.

She reached for the bottom of it. She began.

End of Chapter Eight

Below the third-floor office, below the private dining room, below the dining room and the kitchen and the wine cellar and the war room, the corridor ran west in the dark.

The amber light held steady.

The tunnel did not know what was happening in the room three floors above it.

The tunnel only knew what moved through it—the President's footsteps, the encrypted signal, the slow and irreversible accumulation of truth that moves through a structure the way water moves through old stone: without announcement, without permission, finding every passage that was made for it and, eventually, every passage that was not.

But the building knew.

It had been waiting for Monday morning since the Tuesday in September when a woman had walked out of a burning tower and lost the address of herself and found her way home by the direction the body keeps even when the mind has been emptied of maps.

It had been waiting since Rafi Delacroix had sat down at table four on the first Thursday and opened his notebook to the right-hand page and the left-hand page simultaneously, carrying both operations at once, the financial and the human, the institutional and the private, the thing he was paid to do and the thing he could not stop doing.

It had been waiting since Celestine Arceneaux had looked up at the fourteen-foot ceilings on her first Wednesday and known she was in the right room, though she could not yet have explained how she knew it.

It had been waiting since Tamara pressed a brass plate to the underside of a table and chose four words that were not a sentiment but a law of physics: every truth finds home.

It had been waiting through Thursdays and winters and administrations and wars. Through promotions and retirements and marriages and funerals. Through arrivals that announced themselves loudly and departures that left so quietly that only the building seemed to notice.

Buildings notice more than people think.

They remember repetitions. Footsteps. Silences. The accumulation of ordinary rituals performed often enough that they become part of the structure itself.

And this building, more than most, had become a repository of unfinished things.

Questions waiting for their answers.

Conversations waiting for their final sentences.

Lives waiting for the moment when the pattern became visible.

The amber light remained steady.

The corridor ran west.

Three floors above it, a woman turned another page.

And continued.

Chapter Nine: It's Not My Time

The Thursday after Monday is its own thing entirely.

Dianne had learned this about the operation—that the week had a metabolism, that each day carried the specific residue of the one before it, that a Monday of the kind they had just had changed the temperature of the Thursday that followed in ways that were not operational but human, which were sometimes the same thing and in this building were always the same thing.

She had seen it happen before. A difficult conversation, an unexpected revelation, a guest leaving the room carrying something different from what they had brought into it—those things lingered. They altered the atmosphere in ways that could not be measured but could always be felt by anyone paying attention.

She came down the back stairs at eight o'clock. The room was full.

This was not unusual. The room was always full on Thursdays by eight. What was unusual was the quality of the fullness—the specific temperature of a room in which something was already gathering before the first song, a pressure accumulating in the candlelight and the conversation and the movement of Roy's floor staff that Dianne recognized, from thirty years of reading rooms, as the feeling of an evening that intended to be more than an evening.

Not every Thursday announced itself. Most revealed their nature gradually, over the course of the night. But every so often there was an evening that seemed to arrive already carrying its own momentum, as though something had begun before the first note was played and the room was merely catching up to it.

She noted it, filed it, and continued down the stairs.

She passed Celestine on the floor near table eleven. Celestine did not look up from the wine she was pouring. But her left hand—the hand not holding the bottle, resting at her side in the easy posture of a server mid-service—turned once at the wrist, a small rotation, the gesture of a woman acknowledging a presence without announcing that she was acknowledging it.

Dianne continued to the bar and took her position.

From there she watched her room, letting her eyes travel across the tables, the candles, the servers moving through the aisles, the guests settling into the familiar expectancy that arrived before the music. Nothing appeared out of place. Nothing required intervention.

And yet the feeling remained.

Something was gathering.

Seymour had not told anyone what was coming.

This was the prerogative of a bandleader who trusted his musicians completely and who understood that the best performances were the ones that arrived without the weight of expectation — the ones the band found together in real time, in the room, in response to what the room was asking for. He had told Freeman on Wednesday.

Just Freeman.

He had called him at seven in the morning — the hour Freeman was always awake, the early riser's discipline of a man whose Pentecostal upbringing had put him in a pew at six AM every Sunday of his childhood and who had kept the hour even after he had set down everything else the pew required — and said: "Thursday. I need you on the second song. Not the guitar. Not the harmonica."

Freeman had been quiet for a moment. "The voice," he said.

"The voice," Seymour said. "And I need *It's Not My Time.*" Another moment.

“The sixty-five version or the seventy?” Freeman asked.

“The seventy,” Seymour said. “The Delta arrangement. The one without the brass.”

“Just the voice,” Freeman said.

“Just the voice and what’s underneath it,” Seymour said. “I’ll handle underneath it.”

Freeman had said: “All right.”

He had not asked why.

He never asked why when Seymour called at seven in the morning with a song.

He had learned across years of Thursday evenings that the why was always in the room and always visible by the time the song was needed, and that the preparation required was not intellectual but physical — the preparation of a singer going into something that was going to cost something, the morning of the long distance runner who doesn’t think about the finish line but about the quality of the breath.

He had spent Wednesday and Thursday morning with the song. Not rehearsing it. Living inside it.

Finding the room where it lived in him — which was a different room than the room where *St. James Infirmary* lived, a different room than *The Weight* or *Crossroads* or the Cajun waltzes that lived so close to the surface they barely needed finding. This song lived deeper. It lived in the place where a man went when he was willing to say the hardest true thing without armor, in the place that his Shreveport grandfather had called *the bottom of the well*, which was the place where you went when the singing was not performance but testimony.

He was ready by Thursday morning.

9:47 PM The first song had been *Autumn Leaves.* Seymour's standard opening — the song that calibrated the room, that brought the conversation down and the attention up, that said to the forty-two guests in the dining room: *you are here now, the week is behind you, this is what the next three hours are going to require of you, which is your full presence, which is the only currency this room accepts.* Dianne had not sung the first song.

She had stood at the bar and watched the room receive it.

She had been doing this for four days — standing at the edges of things and receiving them rather than managing them, which was new, which was the change that Monday morning had begun. The file was still open on her desk upstairs.

She had not finished it. She was reading it at the pace that the material required, which was the pace of a person who had spent thirty years studying the architecture of trauma and understood that the approach needed to be incremental, lateral, respectful of the distances that remained.

She was reading herself home. She had time.

The building was not going anywhere.

She watched the room receive *Autumn Leaves* and felt the gathering that she had felt when she descended — the temperature building, the pressure in the candlelight that meant the evening was moving toward something she had not yet identified but that Seymour had seen, which was sufficient.

She trusted Seymour's vision of an evening the way she trusted his vision of an operation. They were the same vision.

The first song ended.

The room settled.

Seymour let the silence run a beat longer than usual. Then he looked at Freeman.

Freeman stood up.

He set down his guitar — carefully, the way he set down everything he cared about, with the full attention of a man who understood that the objects a musician lived with were not equipment but partners, that the guitar had given him everything it had every Thursday for two years and deserved to be set down gently. He placed it on the stand. He straightened.

He walked to the center of the stage.

He did not take the microphone from the stand.

He stood beside it — the microphone at his left shoulder, his hands at his sides, the posture of a man who was not performing yet but was becoming ready to, which is a different posture entirely and which the room felt the moment he assumed it.

The conversations at the tables did not stop immediately. They slowed.

The way conversations slow when a room has shifted and the people in the room have not consciously registered the shift but their bodies have — the gradual turning of heads, the wine glasses lowering without being set down, the specific quality of a dining room in transition between two temperatures.

Seymour played one chord.

A single chord. Open, warm, rooted in the bass, carrying in its voicing the specific tonality of the Delta blues — not jazz, not the Georgetown standards the room knew, something older and further south and more honest in the way that things are more honest when they come from a place that had very little to gain from dishonesty.

The chord hung in the air of the fourteen-foot room. Jerome brushed the snare once.

A whisper. The sound of something beginning.

Stephon brought the Hammond in at the lowest register — not the full Leslie-cabinet swell of a Hammond at volume, but the basement of it, the subsonic warmth that you felt in the chest before you heard it with the ear, the sound of the instrument breathing in.

Dixie found the root on the upright bass. One note.

Held.

The room was quiet.

Freeman took the microphone.

He began without preamble. No announcement, no introduction, no the-next- song-is. He simply began — the voice arriving out of the room's silence the way a voice arrives in a church when the congregation has finally found the stillness it was moving toward, when the preparation is complete and the thing itself can come.

Lord I've walked through the valley And I've stood at the edge of the flame I've seen the faces of the ones who didn't make it And I came back just the same Freeman's voice on this song was not the voice he used on St. James Infirmary.

That was the voice of ceremony.

Of ritual.

The voice that carried the weight of tradition and the dignity of the dead. This was something rawer. Closer to the bone.

The voice of a man from Shreveport who had grown up in a Pentecostal church where the music was not art but need, where people did not sing because they had been trained to or because the song was beautiful but because the alternative was silence and silence was not survivable.

Where a song was sometimes the only bridge between despair and another day.

The voice of testimony.

Something held me back from the darkness Something turned me from the door I don't know the name of what kept me But it's kept me before Seymour's right hand found the melody underneath—not leading it, not announcing it, simply present beneath it the way a current is present beneath the surface of a river, doing the work of movement without requiring the surface to acknowledge it. The melody was there if you listened for it.

And if you did not, it carried you anyway.

His left hand walked the bass line with the patience of a man who had been playing since before he could reach the pedals and who understood that the left hand's job in this music was not to accompany but to hold.

To hold the ground.

To hold the shape.

To hold the song steady while the voice went searching.

Jerome had set down his brushes.

He was playing with his hands—the flat of his palm on the snare in the slow, open pulse of the Delta rhythm, the sound of it almost a heartbeat, almost a footstep, the sound of a man walking and still walking and not yet arrived but still walking.

A pilgrim's rhythm.

A survivor's rhythm.

The rhythm of someone who has every reason to stop and keeps moving anyway.

The snare spoke softly beneath Freeman's voice.

Not marking time.

Marking distance.

One step.

Then another.

Then another.It’s not my time Lord it’s not my time I stood at the crossing and the crossing turned me loose It’s not my time At table four Rafi had stopped writing.

He had been on the right-hand page — the Bethesda consulting firm, the grey sedan’s registration, the third chain of the vehicle operation that he and Seymour were still mapping toward its institutional origin. He had stopped in the middle of a line and set down his pen and was looking at the stage with both hands flat on the notebook, the posture of a man who has been reached by something and is allowing himself to be reached by it rather than managing the reaching.

He was thinking about a North Tower.

He was thinking about eight forty-six and eight forty-seven.

He was thinking about the eleven minutes to Frenchmen Street and the specific and irreplaceable shift from belief to knowledge that he had experienced in the doorway of Preservation Hall — the release of something held so long the holding had become the condition, become what normal felt like, become the thing he didn’t know he was carrying until it was gone.

He was thinking: *she walked out.* He was thinking: *she walked out and the record didn’t have her walking out and I believed the record was wrong and I was right and she walked out.* He was thinking: *it was not her time.* He looked at the stage.

Freeman’s eyes were closed.

They were closed the way his grandfather's eyes closed when he played the fiddle — the old man in the Pentecostal church in Vermilion Parish who had taught Freeman before he taught him anything else that music of this kind required you to put down the part of yourself that watched and managed, that the song needed all of you and the watching part of you was the part it needed least.

I've carried the names of the ones who went before me I've kept them like stones in my chest And I've asked the Lord what the difference was between us Why I was kept and they were blessed But maybe the keeping is its own kind of blessing Maybe the living is the work Maybe the ones who get turned from the darkness Have got a harder road to walk Stephon had brought the Hammond up a register.

Still not the full register—still held in reserve, the instrument's full voice banked like a fire in an enclosed space, the warmth of it filling the room without yet lighting it, promising something larger still to come.

He had the lower manual running the chord and the upper manual playing the countermelody in the octave where Hammond lived closest to the human voice, where the two sounds became almost indistinguishable from each other, where a listener's body did not always know whether it was hearing a man or an instrument and decided, correctly, that the distinction did not apply tonight.

The Hammond was no longer accompanying the song.

It was inside it.

Breathing with it.

Answering it.

Dixie had come off the root.

She was walking the bass now—the specific, unhurried walk of an upright bass player who has found the song's internal logic and is moving through it at the song's pace rather than the tempo's, which were not always the same thing and in this music were rarely the same thing. The tempo belonged to the musicians.

The pace belonged to the truth the song was trying to reach.

The bass in the Delta tradition was not a timekeeper. It was a witness. It moved alongside the voice the way a witness moves alongside a testimony—present, patient, confirming the ground without needing to direct the direction.

Without needing to lead because it already knew where the song was going.

Each note arrived with the quiet certainty of a person nodding in recognition.

Yes.

That happened.

Yes.

Keep going.

Yes.

Tell it all.

And beneath Freeman's voice, beneath Seymour's Hammond and Jerome's restrained snare, the bass continued its measured walk, carrying the song forward not by pulling it but by remaining beside it, faithful to the path and attentive to every step.

Dianne was at the bar.

She had her hands on the bar top — both palms flat, the posture she had assumed without noticing she had assumed it, which she noticed now and did not change. She was looking at the stage. She was looking at Freeman standing at the microphone with his eyes closed and his hands at his sides and his voice carrying something into the room that she recognized the way she recognized the kitchen with yellow walls and the open lowercase a and the feel of a cup held with both hands because the cup was warm and she liked the warmth of it.

She recognized it from the inside.

The clinical vocabulary arrived and she let it arrive and then she let it go, which was new, which was something she had not been able to do until Monday morning and which she was practicing now with the deliberate patience of a woman who understood that a new capacity, like a recovering muscle, required use to become reliable.

She let the clinical vocabulary go. She let the song be what it was.

It's not my time Lord it's not my time I stood at the crossing and the crossing turned me loose It's not my time She knew the crossing.

She had not known she knew it until this moment, until Freeman's voice named it in the language of the seventy blues, the Delta arrangement, the voice of a man from Shreveport testifying in a dining room in Georgetown for forty- two people and one woman at the bar who was receiving it not as a performance but as a fact about herself that she had been building toward for twenty-two years.

She had stood at the crossing.

Eight forty-seven on a Tuesday in September. The crossing had turned her loose.

She had walked out.

She had not known why she walked in the direction she walked. The body had known. The body had been knowing the direction home since it was seven years old and had spent Sunday afternoons on a bar stool on Chartres Street and had learned the feel of a room that was yours and the feel of the direction that led back to it.

She had walked out.

It was not her time.

She pressed her palms flat against the bar top and looked at Freeman and let the song do what it was doing, which was the thing that the songs she had chosen for this room had always done when she stopped managing them and let them work—the deep excavation, the arrival at the truth that lived below the available surface, the specific and irreversible process of a woman being returned, one Thursday at a time, to the self the crossing had tried to keep from her.

The self that had walked out.

The self that had survived.

The self that had kept moving long after it understood how close it had come to stopping.

No one knows the weight of the borrowed time they're living No one knows the account of what they owe But I've been paying it forward in the only currency I carry Which is showing up and letting the living show Freeman opened his eyes.

He looked at the room—not at any single person, not at Dianne at the bar or Rafi at table four or Celestine in the service corridor where she had stopped moving and was standing with her tray at her side and her eyes on the stage and twenty-two years of her own borrowed time visible in the stillness of her.

He looked at all of it.

At the forty-two guests who had come to Georgetown on a Thursday evening for dinner and music and had found themselves, without choosing it, in the presence of a song that was not asking them to feel something but was telling them what they already felt, which is the only thing the blues has ever done and the only thing it has ever needed to do.

A reminder rather than a revelation.

A naming rather than an argument.

He looked at his room.

His voice dropped.

Not in volume. In register. In the quality of it—from the chest voice to the place below the chest, the bottom of the well, where his grandfather had sent him the first time and where he now sent himself without instruction because he knew the way, because the road had been traveled often enough to become instinct: It's not my time Lord it's not my time I stood at the crossing He stopped.

A full beat.

The room stopped with him.

Jerome's palm on the snare. Stephon's Hammond breathing. The bass note held.

Nobody moved.

Then, quietly, with the absolute authority of a man who had carried a song all the way to its bottom and was now speaking from there, Freeman said—not sang, said, the speaking tone of the Delta preacher at the end of the testimony, the voice that has gone past music into something that music was always trying to become: "And the crossing turned me loose."

Another beat.

The words settling.

Finding their places.

It's not my time.

Seymour's hands came off the keys. Jerome lifted his palm.

Stephon let the Hammond exhale—the Leslie decelerating, the sound moving from warmth to silence the way a fire moves when you stop feeding it, not going out but going down, still present, still warm, simply no longer requiring the room to hold it.

Dixie let the bass note find its own ending.

Not cut off.

Not resolved.

Simply allowed to arrive where it had been heading all along.

And then there was silence.

The real kind.

The kind that follows truth when nobody wants to be the first person to move.

The song was over.

The room did not applaud immediately.

This was the room's highest tribute — the moment before the applause, the held breath, the communal pause of forty-two people who have been taken somewhere and are still there, still in the song's country, not yet ready to return to Georgetown and the dinner table and the wine glass and the ordinary geography of a Thursday evening in October.

The former Secretary of State, at table nine, had his hands folded in his lap and was looking at the floor the way people look at the floor when they are experiencing something they want privacy for, something they have no intention of explaining to anyone else.